973.31
B   BLACKBURN, JOYCE
       GEORGE WYTHE OF WILLIAMSBURG

                        COPY 1

San Mateo Public Library
San Mateo, CA 94402
"Questions Answered"

 PRINTED IN U.S.A.

GEORGE WYTHE
OF WILLIAMSBURG

George Wythe. Watercolor portrait by Henry Benbridge, c. 1770.
Courtesy of the R.W. Norton Gallery, Shreveport, Louisianna

George Wythe

OF

WILLIAMSBURG

JOYCE BLACKBURN

HARPER & ROW, PUBLISHERS

NEW YORK, EVANSTON, SAN FRANCISCO,
LONDON

SAN MATEO PUBLIC LIBRARY, SAN MATEO, CALIFORNIA

GEORGE WYTHE OF WILLIAMSBURG. Copyright © 1975 by Joyce Knight Blackburn. All rights reserved. Printed in the United States of America. No part of this book may be used or reproduced in any manner whatsoever without written permission except in the case of brief quotations embodied in critical articles and reviews. For information address Harper & Row, Publishers, Inc., 10 East 53rd Street, New York, N.Y. 10022. Published simultaneously in Canada by Fitzhenry & Whiteside Limited, Toronto.

FIRST EDITION

Designed by Sidney Feinberg

Library of Congress Cataloging in Publication Data

Blackburn, Joyce.
  George Wythe of Williamsburg.
  Bibliography: p.
  Includes index.
  1. Wythe, George, 1726–1806. I. Title.
KF363.W9B55   347'.73'2234 [B]   75–9327
ISBN 0–06–060791–2

75 76 77 78 79 10 9 8 7 6 5 4 3 2 1

COPY I

FOR

Kathryn Pace Cameron

CONTENTS

ILLUSTRATIONS

WHAT IS PAST IS PROLOGUE

•

George Wythe's precise and graceful signature preceded the names of Richard Henry Lee and Thomas Jefferson on the Declaration of Independence.

George Wythe

Even though Wythe added his name in the autumn of 1776 rather than on July 4, it heads the list of Virginia signers.

To his contemporaries—Franklin, Washington, Adams, Rush, Randolph, Madison—George Wythe was truly a symbol of integrity in the colonies, a progressive, forward man whose theories were particularly intoxicating to his devoted pupil, Thomas Jefferson. As a young man Jefferson consulted Wythe in matters of both law and taste, and as president he called Wythe "my earliest and best friend."

Yet, while Jefferson's historical significance thrives, George Wythe's has become mysteriously indistinct. History texts throw little light on his obscurity since from earliest grades American students are acquainted with only the popularized founders of their country. But in 1775, when Wythe arrived in Philadelphia for the Continental Congress, everyone knew him—if not personally, by reputation.

That he remains a stranger to the majority of us, nettles my curiosity because present-day biographies of other colonial patriots mention Wythe frequently but in such passing, vague terms the references amount to a conundrum within the restraints of known facts. This book, while not a formal biography under any pretext, seeks to interpret George Wythe, the Revolutionary idealist, in the hope that his compassionate spirit and pursuit of excellence will enlighten our own values in this perplexing and decisive moment of American history.

When we visit Mt. Vernon, we sense the tranquillity Washington described upon looking across the Potomac from the veranda. At Monticello, we all but hear Jefferson's violin, the wide-ranging conversation with afternoon callers. At Montpelier, we imagine Madison and Dolley racing up the gravel path or looking through their telescope at the Blue Ridge.

In Williamsburg, Virginia, stands the Wythe House, one of the few colonial buildings which was intact when the restoration of that town began. To me, this house strongly suggests the simplicity and elegance of the man Wythe even though he did not design or build it. It was the work of his father-in-law, an architect of considerable fame, whose taste must have complemented that of the Wythes since they occupied the house for over thirty years.

From the time of my first visit in 1937, the Wythe House has been my favorite exhibit in the restored colonial capital. I was seventeen then, and the intense impression was deep-seated, drawing me back again and again through the intervening years. And every visit provoked questions about the origins of the man who lived there—questions which cannot be fully satisfied because he wrote so little about himself for posterity.

Jefferson pleaded with his friend to keep biographical notes, but Wythe did not, and even his extant letters are not collected in a single volume. Ignorant of this at the time, I began filing away any information I happened onto, and as the file grew, so did the mystery of Wythe's ambiguity. I could not go to the library and find a biography of George Wythe (pronounced *with*, by the way). That puzzled me as long ago as the late thirties when I lived on Wythe Parkway, since my father was pastor of the

Wythe Parkway Baptist Church of Hampton, Virginia. Nearby was the George Wythe Junior High School. On Kecoughtan Road, then the main highway connecting Hampton and Newport News, there was a historical marker. I remember pulling off the road for a close look.

WYTHE'S BIRTHPLACE

EIGHT MILES NORTH GEORGE WYTHE
REVOLUTIONARY LEADER AND
SIGNER OF THE DECLARATION OF
INDEPENDENCE, WAS BORN, 1726.

The sign, placed there by the Conservation and Development Commission, was No. 85-W, and it bore the official state seal of Virginia. Reportedly, the original design of that seal had been Wythe's. I drove on calculating where "eight miles north" would be—the Air Force Base at Langley Field, that's where it would be. To learn that Langley encompassed the site of the signer's birthplace came as a frustrating surprise. Langley Field was off-limits to me, and with the subsequent U.S. entry into World War II, security at the base tightened. Civilians understood little about the build-up of coastal defenses. We noted the construction of runways and testing apparatus at Langley, but mostly we just fantasized about swashbuckling pilots in boots and leather jackets roaring off to England in P-38s. *Strategic* was the word always connected with Langley then, precluding any search for historical sites. Hamptonians must content themselves with the mystique of the Wythe family in the local courts. I knew that George, the greatest jurist of them all, had presided at the Elizabeth City County courthouse in old Hampton through the period, 1746–70, and references to the Wythe Magisterial District continued. However, no one seemed to know enough about the flesh-and-blood Wythe to breathe life into his legend.

It was not until 1971—having spent thirty years in another part of the country—that I was finally taken to the site of George Wythe's family plantation "eight miles north" of Hampton. He had called the place Chesterville, and it was at Chesterville that

I began to "feel" the reality of the man—a certain presence, if you will.

In view of a northwest branch of Back River, known now as Brick Kiln Creek, I walked around a fieldstone foundation dating back to the seventeenth century. A simple frame house, eighteen by thirty feet, had once stood on the foundation. I wondered what life must have been like for a boy growing up there. Picturing the place was not easy because a few feet away a hydroplaning test track had been constructed by NACA, parent of NASA. In my frame of mind, the space age and 1726 were incongruous, even though my guide, Dr. Franklin Harris Farmer, was the most ardent student of Wythe's life I had ever met, and Dr. Farmer was/is a biologist for the National Aeronautics and Space Administration at the famous Langley Research Center.

He explained that the house site had been uncovered accidentally when the bed for the hydroplaning test track was bulldozed through the high ground there. This discovery had galvanized a concentrated effort by the Langley Research Center Historical and Archaeological Society to assemble an invaluable Wythe-Chesterville archive. In 1973, the society realized its dream of getting the primary house site and surroundings entered in the National Register of Historic Places. At last Chesterville is a documented landmark, and there can be no doubt that George Wythe's attachment to the place was real indeed.

To the east is the salt marsh, the same vista he knew from childhood. About a quarter of a mile beyond is the creek, a natural boundary of the plantation as well as the boundary between Elizabeth City County and York County to the north. A saucer-shaped radar structure, the main receiver for the pioneer Greenbelt-Goddard tracking station in the earliest space experiments, the nerve center for all pertinent data, stands like a scarecrow at the creek's edge. To the south looms a giant lunar-landing gravity simulator, two hundred fifty feet high, set on massive concrete supports where the Wythe carriage road once passed.

Among his numerous accomplishments, George Wythe was advanced in the pursuit of the natural sciences and mathematics. Perhaps he would be pleased to know that space monuments surround his birthplace. But while such a bridge between his era and ours lends an almost poetic awareness of the relativity between time and space, I confess a sense of loss as well. Time is often just a word for dissolution. And the engineering wonders of the space age do not unlock the secrets of Chesterville. We will never know enough about the place nor about Wythe's life there.

I could dream about it, of course, standing on the knoll ten feet above sea level where the house had been. The April smells of wild onions and mud banks at low tide have not changed. Wax myrtles die down and sprout again where the plantation boat landing must have been. I stoop to touch the bricks recently excavated—stacked, unused, as though just removed from the kiln to dry. The fog still billows in, and with it comes a sensation of being suspended and feathery. I had never quite escaped the spell of Tidewater Virginia, but at Chesterville it overtook me, concentrating my interest, my emotion on an almost forgotten man whose significance cannot be disguised even in the bleak atmosphere of technology at Langley Research Center. Wythe's pronounced pride of ownership was rooted in this place. The family's influence and power derived from it.

Should you visit Chesterville, you, too, may be stunned by the irony that this country's earliest feats in space exploration are already perpetuated in countless books, on tapes and films, while so little has been recorded about George Wythe whose exuberant mind and spirit helped shape the beginnings of America's unique experiment in the government of a free people.

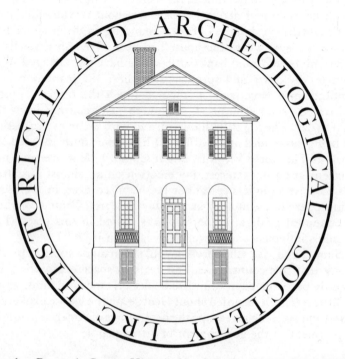

Langley Research Center Historical and Archeological Society Seal showing the house at Chesterville which was built by George Wythe in 1771. *Seal designed by Charles W. Watson, Jr.*

GEORGE WYTHE
OF WILLIAMSBURG

I

ROOTS

•

The Wythes of Chesterville plantation and the Walkers of Hampton in Elizabeth City County, Virginia.

In an old patent book, a land grant is confirmed and described by Sir William Berkeley, Virginia's royal governor in 1676, as "lying and being in the County of Elizabeth Citty at the head of little Pequoson creeke. . . . butting N.W. on the land of Mr Tho Wythe."

Whether or not Thomas was the first Wythe to come to America cannot be proved. He is the first known colonial ancestor of George Wythe, and he settled permanently in Elizabeth City County, adding small parcels of land to his original holdings. From a deed dated 28 March 1691, we learn that this Thomas Wythe, First, purchased "a certaine tract of land or plantation conteyning two hundred and four acres" for fifty pounds sterling. The deed refers to "our Soveraign Lord and lady King William and Queen Mary," the rulers to whom Virginians then swore allegiance.

Out of a primeval setting of creeks, marshes, and forests of virgin gum, ash, sapling oaks and sassafras, farmer Wythe accumulated land, battling for the necessities of existence and transforming wilderness into a fertile kingdom over which he alone ruled. Out of the soil sprang everything good, all profit, as well as loss and disaster. Weather, tobacco, grain, pasture, livestock were his world ringed by untamed nature.

A 1691 deed lists "houses, edifices, buildings, fencing, orchards,

1

gardens," on the property, a substantial gain in one decade of struggle. But deeds did not mention alertness to the quick coastal temperature changes, the tearing winds off the bay, the deer and wolves that ventured forth from the dark woods at twilight. A farmer must be ever watchful, if his reward was to be more than ownership. Contentment could not be conveyed in a document, nor could the instinct for nature's largesse—the black duck and turkey and fox and rabbits in the fall; the large, bony shad in the spring. The Wythes considered the shad roe a delicacy and usually gave the flesh to the slaves; in summer, trout and spot were eaten fresh and salted down for future winter breakfasts; crabs and oysters were fed by the tides, unpolluted, abundant; scaly bark nuts and persimmons and scuppernongs and wild celery in the marsh were hunted in games the children played; and from the apple orchard cider and brandy and vinegar were distilled for cooking and for medicine. These gifts changed little through succeeding generations. But Thomas Wythe, First, mastered wildness only through immense effort, and in the process, attained dignity.

By virtue of his landholding, George's great grandfather was designated Thomas Wythe, Gent., a title of status at a time when an upper class of property owners was developing; assured of holding office, they *were* the local government. Wythe, a justice in the Elizabeth City County court, passed along that position to his heir, Thomas, Second, as surely as he left his land and "foure hogsheads of sweet scented tobacco containing six hundred roots each."

Land, tobacco roots, and authority were inherited by succeeding generations and were innate elements in the background of George Wythe. The history of Elizabeth City County was inseparable from that of his family. He knew that Thomas, Second, had died in his twenties, which meant that George's own father, Thomas, Third, upon reaching his maturity had assumed responsibility for the family, their land, and county office. He, too, had been a justice.

The local governing system was inchoate. The king's administrator, the royal governor of Virginia, simply acted upon the recommendations of county bigwigs when he appointed justices. Justices determined the law governing the organization of the community. They were not men of common social standing, rather, they were the colonial bourgeoisie—men of property who, in effect, passed around the various select offices among themselves. From their closely knit fraternity, they chose the sheriff, and George's father, Thomas, Third, was given a turn in that all-important administrative job. The Wythes were among those families who kept county affairs under their control, and in all fairness to these relatively few, they probably were the most qualified.

For one thing, their class was exposed to learning. They could afford to import books and the social graces from England. While there were no schools of law, these gentlemen read law and debated it, even in the small county of Elizabeth City. Civil law, *jus civile*, was a common topic of conversation, and Sir Edward Coke, once called by the House of Commons *Monarcha juris*, king of the law, was quoted with the same reverence as were the Psalms.

While such an unrepresentative governing body scarcely suggests equality, the justices were usually leaders of ability who appointed lesser officials, supervised them, levied tithes, and made decisions related to the public welfare—building, surveying, licensing, sentencing criminal cases. Judging by the fact that his peers twice elected him to the House of Burgesses, the colony's representative branch in capital Williamsburg, Thomas Wythe, Third, was prominent among the justices. Furthermore, he enlarged the family estate at Chesterville and owned one of the two wharves on nearby Hampton's busy waterfront. He was also a vestryman of St. John's Church located then on the west side of that town. Unfortunately, he did not live to witness son George following in these Wythe traditions. George was only three when his father died; nevertheless there can be little doubt that he was thoroughly taught about his father's character and illustrious public record because during the first sixteen years of George Wythe's life the major influence was his mother.

Although Margaret Wythe was from a family of importance,

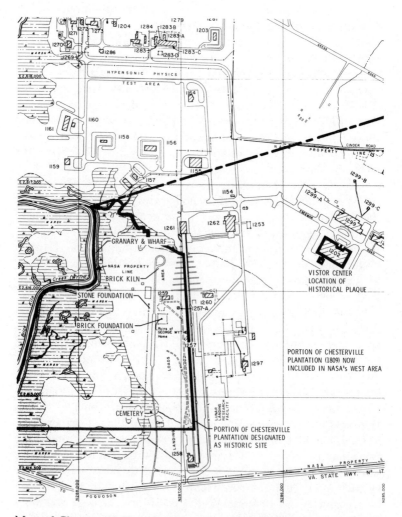

Map of Chesterville/Langley Research Center grounds. *Reproduced by permission of the LRC Historical and Archeological Society.*

it did not belong to the planter class. Her grandfather, George Walker, gained quite a reputation while a young man for skillfully piloting foreign ships through the mouth and channel of the James River, probably on up river, too, past Newport News, where plantation wharves were serviced. Captain Walker knew every inlet of what is still called the lower peninsula—a peninsula between the James and York rivers. The deep waters of the rivers join Chesapeake Bay. Small wonder that the Indians called the Chesapeake, *Mother of Rivers;* the Spanish, *Madre de Aquas.* The waters flowing from it into the land are estuaries and can be navigated merely by the strong push of the ocean tides.

The Walker home was in Hampton, a town established by an act of the Royal Assembly in 1680. The area referred to as Kecoughtan by Indian founders and Elizabeth City by Englishmen was finally designated Hampton, honoring a member of the Virginia Company, the third earl of Southampton. As early as 1607 colonizers had dropped anchor nearby, and white men began settling there, giving credence to the claim that this is "the oldest continuous English settlement in the New World."

Probably fewer than one hundred persons lived in Hampton during the 1680s, and the royal governor's most frequent complaints about the place were the abominable condition of the main county road and the excessive number of "tippling houses." At the waterfront, ships took on fresh water and the county tobacco crops. Sailors swarmed ashore to enliven the business of all of those "tippling houses." During the period when the first three Thomas Wythes were succeeding justices, they handled many cases involving shipwrecks, stolen anchors, and "eloping" servants promised far-off paradises by scheming skippers.

When George Wythe's father was first appointed to the county court, eight pirates were tried. Three were hanged. Colorful tales of the fearless Teach—Blackbeard—were repeated by seamen and citizens. In a bloody battle the king's men had captured him, cut off his head, and sailed right up Hampton Creek with the trophy hung on the bowsprit of their royal sloop. But such barbaric incidents had not diminished Hampton's progress. A center of import-export trade, the town grew into Virginia's princi-

pal seaport during the eighteenth century. The main thorough-
fare, King Street, was crowded on the occasions when everyone
in the county turned out. Farmers brought their crops to the
warehouse on Hampton's river front where they were graded for
shipment to England. A short distance beyond was Point Comfort. Fortified as early as 1609, the Point became an official port
in 1691 where incoming ships were boarded by royal appointees
who inspected cargo and passengers. George Walker, Jr., Margaret Wythe's father, was one of these appointees. He met crews
from England, the West Indies, New York, and from the largest
colonial ports along the Atlantic—Boston and Philadelphia.

Ah, Philadelphia! Shrine of America's Quakers. The captain
was a devout Quaker. Curiously, his wife, the former Anne
Keith, was not. It was a subject of gossip in the county that she
had twice appealed to the Virginia Council in protest against her
husband who would not permit her and their children to attend
Anglican worship. (The unusual combination of Quaker and
Anglican religious precepts will heighten speculation about
George Wythe's "cause," separation of church and government
in the Constitution. It may even explain his rejection of dogma
and "divine rights.")

Like the courthouse, St. John's, the Anglican church in Elizabeth City Parish was another place where folk from all corners
of the county could meet and visit, a natural place for Margaret
Walker first to have met Thomas Wythe. But her father, active
in Hampton's Society of Friends, remained mulish about his
family's preference for St. John's and "the rites of popery."

I suspect that George Walker blamed his wife's father, George
Keith, for the discord. Keith was a noted Quaker evangelist of
forceful personality and learning. With dramatic skill he used
both traits, converting many souls to "the Spirit of Inner Light."
Following the movement's leader, Fox, to prison for heresy had
only added to Keith's heroic image. When Keith brought his
family to America, he became headmaster of William Penn's
experimental Charity School in Philadelphia. Mrs. Keith also
taught in the school. They were pioneer abolitionists, and
George Keith's writings on slavery were later distributed by
Franklin.

But here is the kernel of the Keith-Walker conflict: Keith went back to England for a seven-year stay. Three years earlier while still in America he had, without warning, denounced Quaker mysticism. The abrupt about-face must have created confusion and schism among his followers, especially when the colorful zealot was eventually returned to the colonies as a missionary for the Society for the Propagation of the Gospel, an instrument suspected of furthering the political goals of the crown while at the same time administering the sacraments to the Anglican faithful.

The mighty-willed Scotsman, Keith, seemed a traitor to his former disciples in the colonies, including son-in-law Walker, but when it came to contradictions, Walker had a few of his own. The captain's Quakerism did not allow for military service or oath-taking. Yet, when the government promoted him to a position, under bond to the king, Walker was sworn to "safely keep and preserve all stores of War" delivered to Point Comfort. In order to do so, he was authorized to man cannon and defend the small fort there.

With aplomb, Quaker Walker and Anglican Keith rationalized faith and action while remaining trustworthy, incorruptible servants of the crown. Compromise has been called the pith of diplomacy, and diplomacy would be a trait of George Wythe's long career.

It is interesting to note that once Keith was dead, his daughter Anne Keith Walker no longer quarreled with her husband over their religious differences. The fact is, she entertained Quakers for services in their Hampton home, while continuing in the Anglican communion. Thus the influence of Quaker teaching upon her and daughter Margaret persisted. They both illustrate the independence and intellectual equality which Quakerism allowed women at a time when only men were salaried educators. They were evidently objective beyond the accepted standards of their caste, a progressive factor in the training of Margaret's youngest child, George, who, as an adult would look back and suggest that Quaker principles were organic in his character.

Whether or not Margaret Wythe tutored her son in logic and mathematics is not certain, but he studied the classical languages,

Latin and Greek, with her. She must have been an artful pedagogue; George, a precocious student. I like to think that her gift
for teaching was vividly reproduced in him, as nothing would
ever set his prodigious mind blazing the way teaching did.

Some people claim that the initials GW found on a wall of the
Wren building at the College of William and Mary prove that
Margaret sent her son to school in Williamsburg. But it was said
that students there were pampered in "softness and ease," which
is a basis for argument against his attending the school. If Margaret Wythe doubted the quality of training offered by the college,
her own excellence was reason enough for having kept her
youngest child at home.

A few so-called first Virginia families could afford to send their
sons abroad for schooling. For example, the powerful Mann Page
attended Eton and St. John's College, Oxford. Prominent as the
Wythes were in Elizabeth City County, they were atypical of the
planter class north of the peninsula who amassed great fortunes
through land speculation, tobacco and expedient intermarriage.
Chesterville was indeed modest contrasted with the plantation
up the James owned by the rich Byrds. Called Westover, the Byrd
estate had what architects still refer to as the colossal order.
While Chesterville was among the large farms by Elizabeth City
County standards, it did not produce a lavish living for the young
widow, her three children, Thomas, Anne, and George, and her
clutch of indentured servants and slaves. Unlike most widows,
Margaret Wythe did not remarry for practical reasons of support
and protection; she was more impressed by humane concern than
by wealth.

This heritage was to grow and flower in George Wythe, who
became known in the thirteen colonies as the American Aristides
—a truly just man.

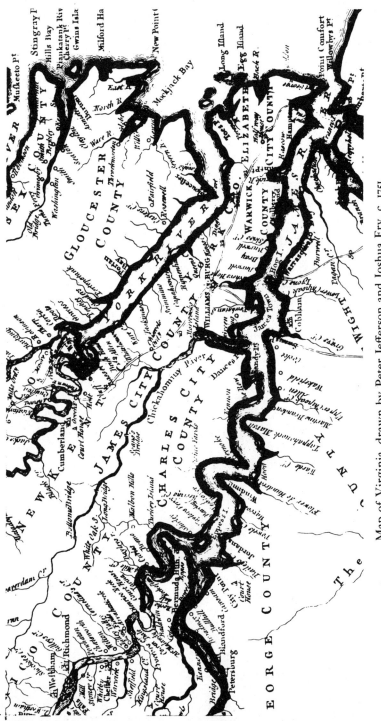

Map of Virginia, drawn by Peter Jefferson and Joshua Fry. c. 1751.

II

APPRENTICESHIP: 1742-1748

•

George Wythe, practicing attorney. Young love and summer death. At work in Williamsburg.

Most of the available facts about George Wythe's early life have to do with his genealogy and the general history of Elizabeth City County in Virginia. I find myself arranging and rearranging them the way one puts a tough jigsaw puzzle together —lining up the outside edges first and then working toward the center.

At sixteen, George, was sent to study law with his uncle, Stephen Dewey, who was king's attorney for the county of Charles City. Dewey was married to one of Margaret Wythe's sisters, Elizabeth, and their home near Petersburg was George's home during his apprenticeship in the study of law.

Why law was his chosen profession is a matter of conjecture, and yet it seems most logical. He had not only relentlessly studied the ancient languages, which gave him a knowledge of the Greek and Roman orders of society, he had been exposed as a matter of course to the procedures of the county court much the same as today's youth is exposed to sports. By 1739, court day was better attended than any other community event, and there is no reason to think the Wythes were different from their Back River neighbors who looked forward to court day, to seeing friends from "ould Poquoson" and Fox Hill and Mill Creek and Buck Roe in addition to the Hamptonians. The county, Virginia's smallest, was eighteen square miles in size. Everyone was acquainted.

The more wealth and property acquired, the more complicated civil affairs became, and the growing population congregated at the court house for the monthly hearings. Equally important, they caught up on the news. George heard talk about the tobacco yield, the size of oysters at the market, races in Isaac Prilly's field, horses for sale. Court day was also market day, and bargaining for brass skillets and grindstones, linen and feathers was brisk. George would have heard the planters, merchants, craftsmen, and servants discuss "Tithes"—taxes to be levied on public projects under construction in the county. The older justices conversed about what was happening abroad, whether Spain and France would continue backing Frederick the Great in his attacks on Austrian territory. In that event, the English and the Dutch would be forced to help Maria Theresa gain the Austrian throne. Of course, once they walked through the courthouse door, looking official in their wigs and ill-fitting "quoshings," they probably turned their attention to a local problem such as "hoggs." Hampton's main streets were still unsafe from wandering animals. One wild boar could root up an acre of turnips.

Then there were cases concerning "ill designing people who went so far as to tear down the fences of law-abiding property owners in order to lay open their pastures and cornfields," for the purpose of turning loose their livestock after dark.

Disputes over boundaries and wills were endless. And there were sensational punishments handed out to mothers of bastard children and men who cursed the king and slaves who stole from their masters.

Citizens were packed together in the courtroom like tobacco leaves in a barrel, standing throughout the proceedings because the benches at the front were reserved for prominent families. That is where George Wythe would have sat, studying the faces of the eight justices, the sheriff, and the accused who sat on a low stool.

If George was present at the trial of A. Smelt's slave, Ned, he learned that the man had not only stolen grain, he had carried it away—*cepit et asportavit.* Centuries ago in Athens in the time of Draco, the law was said by the orator Derades to have been written in blood. Reasoned prudence had enlightened humanity somewhat through the centuries, and Ned would not hang. But he was burnt in the hand and given thirty-nine lashes at the public whipping post. The law must be a servant of justice. George Wythe knew that the branding and flogging would turn into gruesome entertainment once most of the spectators got drunk.

That was court day in Elizabeth City County. It was the same in Uncle Stephen Dewey's county. Still, an apprentice learned much from firsthand observation, and he could take advantage of his uncle's legal library. George read and probably memorized every abridgement and discourse he came across, digesting such abstruse treatises as Sir Edward Coke's *Institutes.* No matter how forbidding and anachronistic the *Institutes* were, Wythe's mind, alert, fluid as quicksilver, sorted out arguments which honed his reason and discernment to a fine edge.

Stephen Dewey was a busy man, too busy, reportedly, to give George the instruction he expected. Instead, he set the young man to copying tedious documents—wills and deeds and writs, ad infinitum. Hour after hour, George, perched on a high stool at a still higher desk, wrote in the long ledgers. Even for someone with a propensity for detail, it must have been an exceptionally frustrating routine, but there were the books he could study alone and the court sessions to observe and the discussion of cases by lawyer friends of Uncle Stephen. This would have been especially invigorating when George accompanied his uncle in the role of amanuensis to the General Court in capital Williamsburg. There, the ablest men of the colony practiced, and when those gentlemen debated procedures, relaxed in the congenial warmth of a tavern, George may have been allowed to voice an opinion now and then. Gauging the conceits of his superiors, the young man probably said little, but what he did articulate would have crystallized all that he was learning.

By 1746, when he was twenty, lean and erect, his prominent forehead "evincing an uncommon identity," George Wythe had learned enough to pass oral examinations successfully and begin the practice of law.

On June 18 of that year, he was "admitted to plead in this

court." "This court" was in his home county of Elizabeth City. If his mother witnessed the proud moment, such a personal note does not appear in the records. Probably she had died because we do know that soon afterward, Thomas Wythe, Fourth, George's brother, became a justice of the peace, having inherited the entire family estate—the Chesterville plantation and the Hampton property.

Thomas may have needed a competent farmhand more than he needed an attorney. In any case, Chesterville was no longer the same. The intimate rooms in the house surely seemed empty without Mother. Sister Anne had become Mrs. Charles Sweney two years before. Even in those slow-paced times, four years brought many changes; so instead of staying in the familiar low country, George went north to Spotsylvania County.

Compared to Hampton, the Fredericksburg area in Spotsylvania County was crowded and noisy since it had become a colonial crossroads. For years, the English had come up the Rappahannock where their ships lay in close to the wharf, even though the river occasionally froze over. The great diarist, William Byrd II, had long ago predicted that "both Religion and Justice will help enlarge the Place." In other words, once a courthouse and church were built, Sir Thomas Littleton's phrase, *Ung Dieu et ung Roy,* "*One God and one King,*" became "visible." By the time George Wythe was established in Fredericksburg, Byrd's vision had become a reality. "The Place" was expanding.

Stephen Dewey had auspicious connections here. His daughter was married to the distinguished solicitor Benjamin Waller. Wythe probably met Waller through his uncle or cousin, and it was one of the most consequential of encounters. The Wallers were of the elite ruling clique in the Virginia House of Burgesses. William, once secretary to the Royal Governor Gooch, and his son Benjamin were as influential in Williamsburg as in their home county. One of the Waller girls, Mary, was the wife of Zachery Lewis, who, with his brother and son, was also prominent in legal circles. It is easy to imagine the advantages of study and experience Wythe enjoyed in the company of such seasoned leaders. George matured rapidly and in one year qualified to practice law in four Virginia counties—Caroline, Spotsylvania, Orange, and Augusta. (Augusta stretched west beyond what is now the Skyline Drive.)

Over this far-reaching territory, George rode hundreds of miles with Zachery Lewis. For the sake of convenience, he lived in the Lewis home. Apparently the senior attorney was more than host. He became fond of George and treated him as a member of the family. The young man from the southern peninsula must have wondered at his good luck as he was intimately associated at meals and evening entertainments with Lewis' daughter, Anne. He did not have to call upon her in order to "present respects" or win the graces of her parents. Under these circumstances, the conditions for a formal courtship were eliminated, and in no time George and Anne were caught up in a far from private romance.

Known even at this young age for the virtues of devotion and candor it seems unlikely that George courted Anne as a matter of expediency so that her father and uncle would secure him a position in government. That he simply fell in love better suits his extralegal personality and suggests that it was Anne herself who mattered, although almost nothing is known about her.

When George asked Zachery Lewis for his daughter's hand, no one was surprised. December was considered an ideal season for weddings since the traditional twelve days of Christmas were celebrated in the Tidewater with feasts and "illuminations," dances and hunts, and Anglican services. Friends and family traveled from home to home, staying as long as they pleased. Upon the occasion of Anne's marriage to George Wythe, the day following Christmas, 1747, the Lewis guest list must have been impressive. Surely Ben Waller and his wife, Wythe's cousin, were there. Perhaps the widow, Mary Ball Washington, who lived nearby, brought her fifteen-year-old son, George, who was unusually tall and self-conscious.

The wedding festivities lasted three or four days, Zachery Lewis leading the gentlemen in early morning hunts while his wife supervised the preparation of elaborate dinners—wild turkey, ham, beef pies, seafood and hot breads, puddings, tarts, candied fruits, with rounds of homemade apple and peach brandy between courses, followed by male guests rushing out into the winter cold to fire a volley of powder and shot with muskets and pistols.

If traveling jugglers and acrobats were in the vicinity, they may have provided evening entertainment, and always there was dancing to the slaves' fiddles and gourds. The modest, reserved groom, his gray eyes laughing, led Anne in reel after reel while elderly aunts sat clucking away before the great log on the fire. Hospitality was an art, and when the guests departed, they took along recipes and quilt patterns, seeds and hunter puppies, comparing the latest house party with the one before.

After their marriage, George and Anne remained in the Lewis home. With his father-in-law, George rode circuit north and south, east and west, to the borders of settled Virginia territory where frontiersmen were disgruntled and eager to push on, driving the Indians over the Alleghenys. Lewis may have taken the young lawyer by to meet the famed surveyor-politician, Peter Jefferson. Such a visit would have been a blessed change from the primitive courtrooms, the niggling litigation over licenses and boundaries, the debts and "battery" to which they were accustomed.

Legal historians "marvel at the appetite for litigation" throughout the colonies. Neighbors sued over boundaries; merchants, over debts; heirs, over wills; politicians, over elections. Human nature doesn't change; lawyers were as necessary then as they are today.

In their travels, Lewis and his son-in-law forded creeks, pushed through the tangle of wilderness along overgrown trails. When it rained, the trails were axle-deep mud. They slept in crude inns more hospitable to vermin than to barristers, but for George, the advantages offset the discomforts. From the variety of arguments, he learned the multiformity of law. Statutes handed down from centuries of English practice had to be modified and adapted to the primitive needs of the new country, especially near the frontier. The problems and outlook of a small farmer whose children provided his labor were unrelated to the concerns of coastal planters with large acreage and numerous help. Exposure to different levels of society and to each community's customs contributed to Wythe's equalitarian values and to his innovative approach to American law. He learned much, too, from the association with Lewis under these circumstances. Together, they could analyze their courtroom debates and legal theory, discuss personalities and various developments in other colonies. For instance, in Pennsylvania Benjamin Franklin was promoting the need of an organized militia in case England's continuing hostilities with Spain and France and the Indians spread. In the Louisburg campaign of '45, volunteers from New England colonies had helped capture France's fortifications, taking back Cape Breton Island for England, but that country's designs on Canada incited the French, along with their Indian allies, to retaliate. Nothing had really been settled. In the West Indies the British fleet continued attacking French and Spanish ships. If Benjamin Franklin was alarmed by these events, so were other thinking colonists.

When the circuit riders returned from their journeys, they eagerly read Franklin's pamphlets from his American Philosophical Society, along with colonial newspapers. Wythe seldom stopped reading; study had been a habit from childhood. He was said to have grown up with a Greek Testament in his hand, his mother reading the English translation. Perhaps now, his wife, Anne, read with him.

However satisfying their marriage may have been, it ended tragically. August, 1748, was a month of fever and harvest. When the big country houses were redolent of herbs and spices, brandy and vinegar, pickling began. Anne watched over the activities in the Lewis kitchen, watched color pour from the kettles, maize and purple, green and scarlet, horseradish white and walnut brown. But later that summer she fell gravely ill and died.

There are accounts, still repeated, that she died in childbirth and that her husband drowned his grief in dissipation during the lengthy mourning period. Research leads modern historians to suspect George Wythe's quick move to Williamsburg after

Anne's death, and his plunge into the political mainstream as well as his start at building a substantial law practice left little time for wild excesses. His rapidly expanding knowledge and experience indicate that work became the creative expression of his emotions and that the tutelage and companionship of Anne's uncle, Benjamin Waller, were his comfort. Their mutual, sudden grief bound them emotionally.

In the event that Waller was in his home county on business that summer of 1748, he and Wythe could have traveled together down to Williamsburg for the fall session of the Assembly in the capital.

Considered one of the finest legal minds in the House of Burgesses, Waller was an ideal sponsor for his late niece's husband, and the established custom was for a protégé of ability to live in the home of his master so that instruction might be closely supervised and encouraged. Waller already knew Wythe's potential, that he was advanced in Greek and Latin and that he had accumulated invaluable firsthand experience riding circuit. If Waller took Wythe into his household, he would have also employed him in his adjacent office which hummed with clients, students, and colleagues.

Unlike some members of the legislature who came into Williamsburg only for the regular sessions, Benjamin Waller was prominent there between sessions as well. Active in the parish church, one of the busiest attorneys around, he also was a city recorder for a period. His wide association with the colony's politicians would serve his "nephew's" interests and Waller's own. George knew this, too, of course; he was singularly blessed to have Benjamin Waller's recommendation.

Impeccably loyal to the king, George Wythe was an Englishman who revered his native Virginia, the largest of the British colonies. And Williamsburg was the seat of government. We can imagine young Wythe's eagerness on the morning of October 28, 1748, the Assembly's opening day. Following his customary routine, he rose at dawn, bathed by tipping a big tub of cold water which hung overhead, ate a hearty breakfast, then studied for an hour—ethics, agriculture, the Scriptures. With customary attention to his grooming, he shaved and brushed his dark hair, selected a spotless white linen cravat, polished the silver buckles on his slippers. Of spare, medium build, he gave an illusion of height, an effect created by his posture and inner composure. A stickler for punctuality, he would leave in ample time for the prayers read before House committees convened.

From the Waller home on the eastern fringe of town, he would walk past the nearby ruins of Williamsburg's first capitol building. Since the great fire in 1747 only part of the brick walls stood. The burgesses, no longer able to meet there, would be gathering instead in the Great Hall of William and Mary College at the opposite end of the street, the main street named for the duke of Gloucester.

Well known in Virginia because of his own family as well as for his Lewis-Waller connections, it is not likely that George passed shops and homes and taverns unrecognized or that his recent misfortune was not discussed. The townspeople took notice of newcomers on the opening day of the Assembly. Was Mr. Wythe attending that day as a spectator, or did he have political ambitions?

His gray eyes shaded by a new tricorn, his hands clasped characteristically behind him, George strode past the shuttered English Coffee House and Burdett's Ordinary. Inns and taverns provided lodging and entertainment for the burgesses who did not own town houses. More famous, of course, were the Raleigh Tavern and Wetherburn's; that morning the dormer windows and white siding reflected the bronzy October sun. The Printing Office would have been of special interest to George as he looked inside. All Virginians took pride in their first newspaper, the *Gazette*. This was where the paper was composed and printed, but documents of the General Assembly and even money were printed there as well. Another popular shop near the "Market-Place" was Dr. Hay's apothecary. Nearer the college Wythe passed the brick buildings of the Powder Magazine, the Guard House, and Bruton Parish Church where the area's most respected midwife, Catherine Blaikley, had seen to the baptizing of her slaves that very year. On the market square and in the church yard, cattle grazed, the summer grass still thick in patches.

George, with an aura of openness and curiosity, unmindful of glances or whispered comments, was not missing any of the street sounds and sights. He admired the heraldic crests emblazoned on coaches going the same direction he was, coaches belonging to the wealthiest aristocrats in Virginia. Now, the Duke of Gloucester Street was glutted with traffic, but he had also been there when the Assembly was in recess. Williamsburg was peaceful then, almost empty. He found this place altogether pleasing. He liked the simple spacious plan, the atmosphere of the "green country town," conceived a half-century before by Royal Governor Francis Nicholson of classical taste.

Almost a mile long and ninety-nine feet wide, the main street connected the capitol on the eastern boundary with the College of William and Mary at the opposite end, a symbolic link between English law and education. Yes, he would live here. He would some day know every shop, every public building, every home the way a scholar knows the books on his shelves.

Ahead was the college with its great chimneys and cupola high against the sky. He was familiar with the building which antedated the others, its brick face with glazed headers scrubbed by weathering. He had been through the arched entrance many times, just as he had observed General Court debates in the capitol where the most solemn issues, "high offences," of the colonial government were settled. When murderers were brought to trial, aristocrat and plebeian drove in from surrounding counties, some prompted by provincial relish for entertainment, some, by enlightened concern for justice. There can be no doubt that Wythe would have been among the latter, descended as he was from a line of county judges and representatives to the House of Burgesses.

When he arrived this autumn of 1748 for the opening of the fall Assembly, he was not a stranger to the members. For one thing, Benjamin Waller made no secret of his pride in his impressive student and treated Wythe as though he were already included in the privileged company. Having been licensed in the courts of

five counties, George recognized representatives he had met on
the circuit. He must have known some members of prestige because by 11:00 A.M., October 28, he had been made clerk of not one
but two standing committees in the House of Burgesses. Both of
the committees were links between the people and their representatives; the Committee on Propositions and Grievances, as
suggested by the title, was a clearing instrument for the complaints and petitions of the voters. The other committee, Privileges and Elections, dealt with the common issues of ballot
stuffing and contested results.

Modeled on the mother country's order of government,
thought to be the most progressive since Aristotle's concept of
balanced representation, Virginia took pride in the cooperative
authority of the royal governor, the Council appointed by the
crown, and the elected House of Burgesses. We can see the pat-
tern of the British constitution delegating authority to speak for
the entire society—the king (royalty), the House of Lords (nobility), and the House of Commons (all other classes).

In the Virginia House, George Wythe had an excellent vantage
point from which to view and learn the complexities of the
colonial system. He was, from the beginning, more than an on-
looker. A committee clerk was "inside," privy to the intrigues,
the competitive maneuvers of members, and the throne-shaking
decisions of this powerful body, the Virginia General Assembly.

On great rolls of parchment, he would keep the record of the
daily proceedings of his two committees. Benjamin Waller served
on both and could suggest methods and particularities to his
student. The opportunity was one any up-and-coming lawyer
would envy. Significantly, the job left George free after the
morning sessions to build his own legal practice in Williamsburg
and nearby counties.

If work could cure the grief of this twenty-two-year-old widower, George Wythe was determined to try.

III

SWIFT ASCENT: 1748–1760

•

Attorney General and burgess, in that order. Chesterville inherited. Bride, Elizabeth Taliaferro. The Wythe house.

By the time the General Assembly adjourned the fall session of 1748, Wythe was accepting court cases in York and Warwick, two counties south of Williamsburg adjoining his native county of Elizabeth City. He was acquainted with people of the area, and, of course, the people, knowing the Wythe family reputation, trusted him. Court records indicate that he went frequently to Hampton, the Elizabeth City county seat. One of the main stage routes from the capital to Yorktown joined with the Back River Road which passed the home plantation, Chesterville. In the early 1700s, it could take most of a day to ride there from Williamsburg, depending on how long one stopped at the sign of the Swan in Yorktown. More politics and trade were debated at the Swan than in the courthouse across the road. A post rider delivered the *Virginia Gazette* to the inn where it was read aloud to the customers. George may have so favored them when he stopped off to work in the York court.

He most surely hurried to Chesterville after the hurricane of 1749 to make certain that his brother Thomas and the slaves were safe. His sister and her family had moved across the waterway (now known as Hampton Roads) to Norfolk. Wharfs and mills and cabins were swept away by the storm, and if Thomas Wythe's tobacco crop was deposited in the Hampton Warehouse at the time, it was lost, "overflowed with high tides . . ." Even the

21

walls of the fort at old Point Comfort were destroyed by the force
of the sea, and the barracks there were saved only because Captain Samuel Barron had "all the weighty articles they could lay
their hands on" moved to the second story.

Always infested with insects, the peninsula was assaulted by
mosquitoes bred in the wake of the hurricane rains. In spite of
all the smudge pots at Chesterville, clouds of mosquitoes crazed
man and beast. The cattle plunged through undergrowth to
brush off the pests. Cattle died. People died. Fever spread unar-
rested. How long it took the farmers and merchants to recover
is not known, but unlike today's disaster programs, the government provided no relief, even though taxes steadily enriched the
crown. Government must tax, and taxpayers must grumble.

Tax evasion is not a modern practice. The planters with the
largest land holdings were the men grabbing more, steadily acquiring land without bothering to report, so that lawful taxes
often were not collected. Some Virginians had also profited from
trade with the French at the very time their fellow citizens to the
west were menaced by France and her Indian allies.

Neither of these practices sat favorably with Royal Governor
Robert Dinwiddie when he took over the administration of the
colony. Early in 1752, he called the Virginia Assembly into session. Expecting to dispense with the colony's business in a few
weeks, the burgesses became exasperated when the session
lengthened into three months. But the tax evasion issue could not
be settled quickly. The more autocratic the governor's attitude,
the more independent his legislators became. To assert unmistak-
ably the authority Dinwiddie considered rightfully his, he
matched the trickery of the tax evaders with trickery of his own.
It was the governor's duty to sign the patent which made a
government land grant legal, and when Robert Dinwiddie took
office, one thousand applications for patents awaited his attention. The wily governor made the most of the situation; he simply began, in effect, charging for his autograph. For each land
patent signed he would collect a fee of approximately four dollars. This was not a secret maneuver; the upper council of aristocratic loyalists agreed, of course, that the amount was reasonable.

Not so the lower House of Burgesses. *This* tax violated their "constitutional" rights. They had not approved it. Never mind that they had been ignoring the land taxes for years, they were now being taxed without their consent.

The dispute reached a deadlock when Dinwiddie was distracted by an unexpected threat to the colony's safety. He had sent Major George Washington with a letter warning the commandant of the French forces on the Ohio that he was trespassing on English claims. Washington sent back word that the French were unyielding. They claimed the same territory and would fight for it. This meant that the House must immediately vote funds enabling Washington to launch an offensive. The royal governor had not anticipated such a grave matter arising when he began his game of cat and mouse with the burgesses. Now he was desperate. The representatives were hostile.

First, they voted £20,000 for the border war; then without a nod at the lofty council, voted an additional £2,500 for the impudent purpose of sending Attorney General Peyton Randolph across the Atlantic to protest Dinwiddie's "unconstitutional" patent fee before the English Board of Trade. The governor forbade the journey. Randolph paid no attention. Dinwiddie retaliated by dismissing him. As Edmund Randolph wrote in his famous *History*, "The Governor was wounded to the soul, and personal revenge was his weapon. He superseded Peyton Randolph from the office of Attorney General, and appointed George Wythe."

The move from committee clerk to one of the top positions in Virginia's government was astounding, especially since George Wythe was not even an elected member of the House.

Why was he, a clerk, Dinwiddie's choice? Was Wythe's mentor Benjamin Waller behind the appointment? Or had Wythe already shown a disposition suiting him for the role of keeping the lines of communication open between opposing forces?

Not yet thirty, he accepted his quick prominence as though it were his birthright, and when one of the House members died in August, his fellow solons elected him to fill the seat. He was a burgess.

Wythe soon let it be known that he would relinquish the powerful position of attorney general bestowed by the governor the moment Peyton Randolph returned. A calculated as well as a courteous move which assured him of his colleagues' support.

The following year, 1755, Randolph came back from London with a satisfactory compromise in his pocket: A continuation of the governor's land patent fee, combined with restraints on his authority in matters of taxation. Also, Randolph was to be reinstated.

Having made an excellent impression as stand-in attorney general, George Wythe, the twenty-eight year old burgess, was rewarded with appointments to the very committees he had so recently clerked. Due to the favorable combination of events, his distinguished talent and influential friendships, he had swiftly moved into the echelon of decision-makers.

His personal fortunes vaulted in stride with his career when, overnight, he became a man of property. Thomas Wythe, his brother, died without heir, and the family estate of Chesterville passed into George's possession. Besides the plantation, he "inherited" Thomas' position on the Elizabeth City County court, becoming the fifth member of the family appointed by a royal governor to serve what became known as the "Wythe Magisterial District."

In Williamsburg, George's private practice flourished. Among his clients was Robert Carter of fabled wealth. Managing the estate of a gentleman who owned 50,000 acres of rich land assured Wythe of a substantial income, but the status conferred simply by being Carter's attorney was even more valuable. Their association was an advertisement of Wythe's superior ability and, most important, his integrity.

All of these assets made him one of the most eligible young men in the capital, and it was there that he met, courted, and married the cultivated Elizabeth Taliaferro.

Elizabeth's father, Richard Taliaferro, was a wealthy land speculator; consequently he was prominent in political circles as a James City County justice. In Williamsburg, the county seat as well as the colony's capital, Taliaferro was called "our most Skillful Architect." Four miles out of town was the large family plantation, "Powhatan," noted for its mansion of classical proportions.

In town, Taliaferro had designed and built a town house "on Palace Street near the Church." The governor's residence and Bruton Parish Church were prime symbols of English tradition; so the architect had not chosen the site for the town house haphazardly. And when his daughter married George Wythe, Taliaferro made her a present of the house. (*Present* is a misleading word perhaps, as she would not inherit the property until her father died.)

Elizabeth's wedding was a social event, and the sixteen-year-old's match with the twenty-nine-year-old widower, assured of a distinguished future, was, of course, widely discussed.

Elizabeth and her brother, Richard, were the only children of the Taliaferros, and thorough attention had been lavished on their upbringing. Tutored in literature, music, dancing—"the riches of the mind"—Elizabeth was an attractive, intelligent companion. She was accomplished, as were all ladies of her class regardless of age, in the intricacies of managing a household: servants must be supervised efficiently, hospitality planned with diplomatic savoir faire, an atmosphere created in the Wythe House complementary to the master's modest but eclectic habits.

Between the lines of George's subsequent orders for goods from London merchants, we find hints of Elizabeth's preferences —damask table cloths, "elegant" china, "handsome" services of glass, seed catalogs, satin cloaks, and satin slippers "with full high heels."

It is easy to imagine the delightful dimensions added to George's already full life by his young bride, her family, and the house so centrally located in the town he loved. We know that for thirty-two compatible, gracious years, he and Elizabeth resided there, traveling to visit relatives at Powhatan and Chesterville, but always returning eagerly to Williamsburg, the heart of colonial Virginia's government and culture.

The Wythe House (restored) in Williamsburg designed and built by Richard Taliaferro, Wythe's father-in-law, and given to the Wythes as a wedding "present." *Courtesy of the Colonial Williamsburg Foundation*

The ebb and flow of history reflect the microcosmic changes in our individual worlds, from lofty attainment to the sloughs of humiliation, often from acclaim to rejection. George Wythe's first decade in the colonial capital was marked by success, position, a splendid marriage, and acceptance among the elite movers of events.

Nevertheless the folk in his home district were unimpressed, for there, in Elizabeth City County, he lost his first political contest in 1756. Two years later, he tried again and was defeated by a still wider margin. In both elections, he was opposed by the popular Hamptonians, Colonel John Tabb and Captain William Wager. In the 1758 race, Wager attracted ninety-five votes from the freeholders, Tabb, seventy-six, Wythe, eight! Plainly, the local leaders had the edge of having been actively on the scene. George was known in the capital all right, but living there rather than in the home county put him at a disadvantage.

County records indicate that men with military commissions were favored. Their rank in the militia apparently influenced voters, and service in the militia automatically classified a man as "fit and able." Enlisted neither in Williamsburg nor Hampton, George appeared a pacifist compared with his opponents. Furthermore, he may have seemed detached from the ordinary, daily issues on the grass roots level, so absorbed was he in affairs at the capital.

Of course, some peninsula citizens took pride in their native son, while others had reservations about his high and powerful "connections." Among the small farmers and tradesmen, Wythe's reserved personality might have been considered haughty, even his marriage into the urbane Taliaferro family taken as a slight by his critics. Had he thought he was too good for a bride from Elizabeth City County?

Perhaps he lost the elections for a less-complicated reason—failing to provide the quantity of strong drink and refreshment that his rivals did. Voters came to the polls expecting to spend the day, with free food and drink in ample supply. Candidate Wythe, moderate and frugal, may have failed to sense the importance of exchanging a cup for a handshake, a drink for a vote.

George Washington, even after he had become something of a military hero, took pains to keep the 391 constituents in his home county happy with twenty-eight gallons of rum, fifty gallons of rum punch, forty-six gallons of beer, fifty-four gallons of wine—plus a little cider.

Wythe had no military exploits to glamorize his record, nor the campaigner's gift for small talk and flamboyant promises. He was far more authoritative than expedient, and, being a temperate man in the midst of the commonplace excesses, Wythe's defeats on the county level may not be so surprising after all. Taking everything into account, the fact that he *did* win a later election is more extraordinary.

Any trace of idealism about the election process in these United States has long since been erased by events, and with hindsight we now wonder about the true function of that important Committee of Privileges and Elections in the House of Burgesses. Maybe a certain Mr. Johnson was more factual than snide when he described the chicanery of the gentlemen of the House: "You know little of the Plots, Schemes and Contrivances that are carried on there; in short, one holds the Lamb while the other skins." It was one way of saying that preserving the privileges of the ruling few was more important than honest elections, and *they* "looked out for their own."

Wythe, however, was probably not too discouraged by the loss of the election in Elizabeth City County because the public's esteem for him as judge of their court was not in the least affected. Besides, Williamsburg was the center of most of his activities, and among his friends were those men who controlled the powerful College of William and Mary which, small as it was, had its own House representative. This custom began in England where universities sent representatives to Parliament. It was continued in the colony by Reverend James Blair, the Scottish, autocratic founder of the college, who also became the minister of Bruton parish. Combining his influence in education and the established church, Blair was appointed by the crown to the twelve-man Council, and in his old age (1740) exercised his right as the senior member of that body to run the colony during the absence of the royal governor on a military expedition. Blair's attitude reflected that of the king: A man loyal to His Majesty, would be loyal to His Majesty's church as well. Through the years, the power of church and government and the college had become conveniently interwoven.

When George Wythe lost the Elizabeth City County race, the college faculty elected him to the House of Burgesses, succeeding Peyton Randolph who then became the Williamsburg representative. Passing around these choice appointments among a select few simply duplicated the county system on a more sophisticated level. Wythe's new association with the College of William and Mary indicates a conspicuous rise in his power. And this was emphasized still more when he was also made a vestryman of Bruton parish. He was moved into the Assembly after all. Furthermore, he would benefit from the additional key ties to the college and the church.

At thirty-four, despite the political setback in his home county, he could scarcely have hoped for a more propitious standing in the colony's oligarchy.

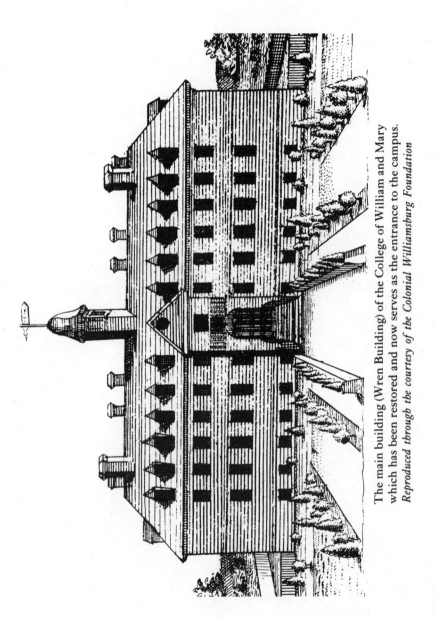

The main building (Wren Building) of the College of William and Mary which has been restored and now serves as the entrance to the campus. *Reproduced through the courtesy of the Colonial Williamsburg Foundation*

IV

FRIENDSHIP

•

Teacher Wythe's "salutary influence" on student Thomas Jefferson. Royal Governor Fauquier's quartet.

While it is well known that the College of William and Mary was chartered in 1693 by King William III and Queen Mary II, another early venture in Virginia education is seldom mentioned. The citizens of Hampton and Elizabeth City County claim that America's first free elementary school was established there in 1635, thanks to the will of one Benjamin Syms who left two hundred acres for the purpose of producing enough income by pasturing cows and supplying milk "for the maintenance of a learned, honest man." This "honest man," the teacher, would instruct the children of the county. As early as 1647, the dairy herd had increased production sufficiently for an adequate schoolhouse to be built. Twelve years later, one of the Wythes' neighbors, Dr. Thomas Eaton, followed Syms' charitable experiment, providing for "the upkeep of a school, 500 acres of land near the head of Back River, 2 slaves, 20 hogs, 12 cows, 2 bulls, sundry farming and household utensils ranging from cheese presses to milk pails."

Eaton's school was to serve the poor, an altruistic enterprise. Not even George Wythe, who would champion free education in the new United States, was more progressive in his community concerns than were Syms and Eaton. By more than two centuries, they "anticipated" in the small county of Elizabeth City the establishment of a free public school system. And the Eaton

31

Charity School and Syms Free School had "a continuous existence" into the nineteenth century. Instructors, licensed by the
governor, were examined and selected by county leaders. We
conclude that they really wanted the lower class to be able to add
and read and write because orphans, bondsmen or apprentices,
and free blacks were enrolled, while the sons and daughters of the
gentry class were tutored by the local Anglican rector. Wythe,
the owner of Chesterville and a gentleman justice of the county
court, supported these unique educational institutions.

When he became more active in the management of Chesterville in 1760, he leased all but an acre of the adjoining Syms School
property. This expanded his holdings to almost 1,000 acres, modest enough compared with those of his clients Carter and Washington, but impressive in the home county. Maintaining the Williamsburg house and the social position he and Elizabeth had
established required more income from his land as well as from
his law practice.

While tobacco remained the principal crop, its growers had to
replace the land it depleted. Those "sweetscented roots" mentioned in Wythe's greatgrandfather's will had been symbolic of
Chesterville's basic economy. The species of tobacco cultivated
there is not recorded, but if it was *N. rustica*, it was mild in flavor
and large-leafed, a strain originated in Virginia. It became
"prime money," the base of currency and credit in the entire
colony. The quality and quantity of the crop a farmer took to the
warehouse for grading and export decided the quality and quantity of goods he could receive from abroad in exchange.

The legacy of tobacco roots was proof of the first Wythe's
patient, back-breaking industry rather than the fertility of Elizabeth City County soil. The eighteen square miles of peninsula
were raked by tides and storms. The sandy earth was far more
favorable to pine woods than to a crop threatened by worms and
fungus, poor drainage, and wet, frosty, northeast winds. Thomas
Jefferson described the culture of tobacco as infinitely wretched,
requiring "a continued state of exertion beyond the powers of
nature to support."

Farming was an enthusiasm which Jefferson and George

Wythe held in common. Both men were descended from British settlers—the Jeffersons in the western hill country, the Wythes in lower Tidewater. Their predecessors wrested land from the wilderness small parcels at a time, turning it into productive acreage. To their descendants, they passed along what has been called "that *feel* of all with which Nature concerns herself"—an intimacy with the exultation and despair of farming, a sense of wonder at growing things, an awareness of life which a man through greed can ruin, or with love can make fertile.

Agriculture and learning would excite Wythe and Jefferson for their lifetimes. Through the years of their friendship they would exchange seed catalogues as well as the *Olympiads* (diaries from the early Christian era, truly esoteric, all but unknown to most scholars).

In 1760, seventeen-year-old Tom Jefferson began studies in Williamsburg, first at the college, then as a private student of George Wythe, now thirty-four. From the beginning of their association there was an extraordinary union of intellect and understanding. Together they explored a universe of ideas, freeing themselves of narrow outmoded tenets by disciplined concentration. Caught up in this common fervor, the age difference did not diminish their friendship. Rather, time enhanced the attachment so that after forty-six years, when Wythe died, the younger man reflected upon his "earliest and best friend," then added a most revealing and moving declaration, "to him I am indebted for first impressions which have had the most salutary influence on the course of my life."

That "salutary influence" included far more than the teacher's passion for law. It included, for one thing, Jefferson's introduction to the social stimulus of the most urbane company, namely that of Royal Governor Francis Fauquier (who had succeeded Dinwiddie), and of Dr. William Small, professor of mathematics at William and Mary.

The Fauquier family, sophisticated and worldly, found Williamsburg provincial. Except for the governor, who, after all had little choice, they soon sailed back to England. Alone in the

Thomas Jefferson as a young man. *Reproduced through the courtesy of the Virginia State Library*

drafty palace, Fauquier could have escaped into his "Binn Cellar" and drowned his boredom in madeira. Instead, he set about establishing a record for efficient administration in the capital, leaning in part on George Wythe who became not only the governor's advisor in colonial affairs, but a favorite dinner partner.

According to Jefferson, Wythe and Dr. Small were "intimate friends," and it was only natural for Fauquier to cultivate two of the most forward minds in town. It scarcely matters how the governor met young Jefferson, whether Wythe or Small introduced them, but they became a notable foursome, dining at the governor's palace and then retiring to the upper middle room where they made both conversation and music.

I can imagine Professor Small, the ruddy Scot, and young Tom Jefferson coming up the Duke of Gloucester Street from the college, turning left at the Palace Green, to stop by for Wythe whose house was the first on the left. From there, the three friends strolled on to the nearby palace where liveried servants admitted them to the great hall with the king's wooden-carved coat-of-arms above the fireplace. Informal on these occasions, Fauquier conceivably called from the stair landing, "Come on up, gentlemen, to the library."

The governor and Small were each in the prime of life, each wise in the ways of the mother country; Wythe, in his early thirties, was already the poised "man of consequence"; and the young Jefferson with long sandy hair and freckled complexion was slender, tall, limber as a candleberry myrtle. In Jefferson's words, the four men formed a "partie quarée." He once remarked, "To the habitual conversations on these occasions, I owed much instruction."

What did they talk about? While their personalities were dissimilar, their pursuits were not. Since they were too liberal in their philosophy to approve of the calibre of education offered by the college, the William and Mary curriculum was probably a topic of disdainful comment. Dr. Small was the only professor who was not a clergyman. The college was controlled by the established church, and one justification for its support was the training of young Virginians for the Anglican ministry. Relatively few of them took to religion, it seems, perhaps in reaction to the secular power centered in the college president who, continuing in the tradition of founder Blair, also served the pulpit of Bruton Parish Church and was the agent or commissary to the bishop of London.

While Jefferson was enrolled, the president was the Rev. Thomas Dawson, whose habitual drunkenness often left both school and church without official supervision, not to mention spiritual guidance. Dawson's predecessors, particularly abstemious James Blair, had at least performed their ecclesiastical duties with sobriety. Nevertheless, they had wielded a disproportionate influence in political decisions and won for themselves material wealth while making converts to the Church of England.

Governor Fauquier was more sympathetic to Rev. Dawson's excesses than to the doctrines of the church. A gourmand, the royal governor delighted in elaborate, intimate dinners, relished betting at the track or at cards with hedonistic abandonment. Since Wythe and his pupil, Jefferson, were almost severe in their diet (they became vegetarians, no less), drank only wine, and that moderately, it is likely that "the four" valued communication more than uniformity of outlook.

This was a period in the colonies, following the so-called Enlightenment in Europe, when many of the intelligentsia quoted Voltaire: "Much to be pitied are they who need the help of religion to be honest men." Francis Fauquier was not a lone doubter in this curious quartet by any means. A quarrel begun in the fourth century between Arianism and the doctrine of Homoousian had been perpetuated in the colonies, and its offshoot, Deism, was the "current heresy." (Only a theologian dare explain the fine points, but Wythe could and did.) An oversimplification would be that Christ was a created being, therefore not God in the fullest sense, a divisive departure from Anglican orthodoxy spelled out in the Apostles' Creed: "I believe . . . in one Lord Jesus Christ, the only-begotten Son of God; . . . Begotten, not made. . . ."

It is probable that Governor Fauquier shared with his three friends his intention to order the creed struck from the liturgy.

What were the reactions of Wythe, Small, and Jefferson when their companion, enthroned in his embellished royal pew at Bruton Parish Church, clamped shut his mouth when his own order was ignored and the creed recited?

Those communicants who attended just to observe Fauquier, the king's representative, noticed and tattled, you may be sure. And did the four at their next gathering, discuss the minister's reasoning, his refusal to eliminate the creed? At the time, they were colonial deists, as were Washington, Franklin, and Adams; their rationale minimized supernatural revelation, in the parochial sense of the word.

While the Williamsburg rector would not obey the meddlesome royal governor, he and fellow ministers certainly did not require complete conformity. Deists were prominent in the local Anglican power structure. Such compromise was a factor in the rise of dissenters and marked a decline in spiritual zeal from the days of George Whitfield's evangelistic tours through the south twenty years earlier. At that time Whitfield, a young controversial graduate of Oxford (not allowed to preach there), attracted huge crowds in the American colonies with his compelling fervor. He had described how "the word did fall like a hammer and like fire" during his sermons, and the Great Awakening led by him had stirred many Virginians. In his opinion, Williamsburg folk were a notable exception. "In these parts, Satan seems to lead people captive at his will . . ." Whitfield wrote. He complained, too, about the small crowds attending his meetings in Bruton Parish Church. To a *Virginia Gazette* reporter, the congregation was "numerous"; the magnetic preacher was "admired and applauded." Later, in a colony "famous for uniformity of religion" (the phrase of an Anglican, no doubt), the passionate Whitfield was accused of spreading Schism. Certainly, from the Church of England point of view, he did just that because his sermons were to inspire Presbyterianism in Hanover County, Baptist churches in Spotsylvania, and missionaries of Methodism who roamed the frontier.

These developments were surely meat for debate among Fauquier, Wythe, Small, and Jefferson who were amused by "emotional religious epidemics."

At ease, within the privacy of the royal governor's own quarters upstairs in the palace, conversation must have echoed the avant-garde attitudes of the most unconventional minds of the eighteenth century. For example, in Swift's satire, *A Tale of a Tub*, the Irish Anglican priest poked fun at the overly pious (although Swift later wrote *Arguments Against Abolishing Christianity*). The comedy, *Le Tartuffe* by Molière was still popular at the time in England because its target was hypocrisy. Montesquieu's *De l'esprit des lois* (The Spirit of Laws), published only a decade before in English compared three forms of government—monarchy, despotism, republic—and set forth a concept of the separation of powers which can be detected in the Constitution of the United States.

Long after the Englishmen Fauquier and Small were gone, Wythe and Jefferson would work to abolish the power of the established church as an agent of the crown. To them, as well as to others who agreed with them, we owe America's religious freedom, eventually spelled out in the Bill of Rights: *Congress shall make no law respecting an establishment of religion, or prohibiting the free exercise thereof.*

I am not suggesting that the convivial companions dwelt only on profound topics. After all, they were intimately acquainted with establishment gossip. The state of the colony's economy was as unstable as today's trade markets. Hour after hour, they must have argued their pet solutions. Professor Small was George Washington's doctor; so he may have confided what medication he was prescribing for the young squire of Mt. Vernon in the event it was something experimental. A student of medicine at Glasgow, Small apparently preferred to teach mathematics and philosophy while at the College of William and Mary, where his lectures made him a favorite with the young men because he was not only eloquent and logical, he was also never dull.

Jefferson possibly passed along the campus news that students must not keep their race horses in town and that a Mrs. Foster had become stocking-mender at the college. Her pay was £12 a year.

There can be little doubt that Francis Fauquier brought up that old conversational standard, the weather. As a member of the Royal Society of London, he kept a detailed log of day to day natural phenomena. Science was at the crest of the wave of the Enlightenment which swept across the Atlantic, engulfing progressive colonial thinkers. Wythe was to become a founding member of Virginia's Society for the Promotion of Useful Knowledge of which Benjamin Franklin was a corresponding member. Like Franklin, Wythe and Jefferson collected throughout their lives all of the scientific apparatus they could afford.

Besides dining and talking, the four indulged yet another avocation, music. Young Jefferson played violin and cello. Did Dr. Small also play violin? The governor, harpsichord? George Wythe, flute? They performed together with more than a passing enthusiasm since ensemble requires "a well-judging Ear" and an exacting sense of rhythm. They were practiced amateurs.

Fauquier owned a library of cosmopolitan repertoire, and the better musicians in the colony performed Handel, Purcell, Corelli, Hasse, and Alberti. (Jefferson once complained about the loss of a half-dozen new minuets, sonatas, airs, duets, and marches; rats had made away with the scores.)

Music, good talk, and informal dining contributed to these gatherings, but it was the highly individualistic personalities of the four men that made their friendship remarkable. We are reminded that almost two centuries before, intellectuals gathered at London's Inner Temple and Inns of Court, where, by association, they taught apprentice lawyers, such as young Jefferson, the social graces—"how to hold one's own in a part song after dinner, how to dance, drink, bow, make a knee before one's betters." In this unaffected Virginia company, age and position seemed of no matter. They met as equals, humane, erudite, specialists in the joys of being.

V

PURPOSE

•

Victory in the home county. Ancient protest. Advanced concerns.

In 1761, Wythe's prestige in the House of Burgesses was acknowledged at last by the homefolk. When he ran for election again in Elizabeth City County, he won.

The number of voters was up to 1,155, almost twice the "tithables" at the time of George Wythe's birth thirty-five years before. Accordingly, the representative's responsibilities were doubled because the increased population required more public services. For example, "In order to get to court, to church, to market, all of the people on the east shore of the peninsula . . . were dependent on the ferry. The traffic was so heavy, one ferryman, John Proby, resigned. A small bridge had been built over Finches' Dam, extending the important Sawyer's Swamp Road to York County.. . ." (This road, still in use today, was known as "the back road to Newport News.")

Judging by a sampling of estates in the home county, Wythe's constituents were progressive and prosperous. One Anthony Tucker had imported a fine desk and twelve new leather chairs. In his will, William Parsons left fourteen slaves and a remarkable assortment of books and *two* "wigg boxes." John Tabb also left a choice library, a complete set of china, and "twelve framed prints"—luxuries appropriate for a justice. But Westwood Armistead's interests were more rural if twenty-four slaves and one dictionary are an indication. His will also included twenty-five gallons of apple brandy and fifty of peach. Like Wythe, who had planted an orchard of one hundred trees on the leased Syms property, Armistead grew fruit in quantity.

Education had become "compulsory"; so the electorate was presumably more informed. They needed an influential burgess in the capital. George Wythe, who was serving on three major committees, and who knows how many *ad hoc* committees, had every qualification.

This must have been one of the most active periods of his life, commuting from his home and his practice in Williamsburg down to Hampton where he "managed" the court rather the way he managed Chesterville plantation—as though he owned it. From niggling in county affairs, his multifarious skills now ranged among major issues in the Virginia government. For one thing, the crown, more determined than ever to keep the French out of the western border region, had balked at subsidizing the whole Virginia militia in the effort. £20,000 spent on military aid must be repaid the English, and Wythe was one of the leaders expected to solve the financial predicament. He was chosen because of his reputation for industry and fairness known throughout Virginia. At the same time, such efficiency can make a man seem mechanical, remote. The professional Wythe may have been a near contradiction to Wythe, the informal companion, the engaging, warm individual his admirers knew. During House debates or while sitting on the bench, he was often accused of long-windedness and undue display of intellect, given to lengthy flourishes of Greek and Roman illustrations. A quote from Homer's *Iliad* or a Seneca *Maxim* might well clarify a point, no matter how obvious the squirming of the burgesses in the chamber.

If this was subconscious exhibitionism, student Jefferson was not among those listeners bored by the careful diction and elaborate phrases. He understood Mr. Wythe. Their teacher-pupil association would stretch beyond the usual two years into five, and throughout those years Jefferson was privy to all of Wythe's legal and political tactics, some of which foreshadowed the eventual independence of the colonies.

A member of the Committee of Correspondence in the House,

Wythe and a colleague were chosen to word a letter of instruction to Virginia's agent in London, William Montague. Montague was, in modern vernacular, a lobbyist for the Virginians who conveyed to the royal government assembled at Westminster whatever was in the best interests of the colony. The method of communication had been devised five years before, and from the beginning, money had been the paramount subject. By printing and circulating her own paper money, Virginia had stirred the ire of the Board of Trade and Governor Fauquier; sterling was the currency of English merchants, not unregulated paper. In effect, Wythe wrote Montague that the English could accept Virginia paper or else.

On the heels of this quarrel, Parliament proposed a tax on two of the most essential imports—madeira and the stamps required on every legal document in order for it to be official.

The Committee of Correspondence instructed Wythe and his associate Robert Carter Nicholas to write a protest against what amounted to taxation of Virginia's internal trade, and in the protest turned up the phrase, "without their consent."

Wythe's thought, and Jefferson's in turn, mirror the philosophy of John Locke, who had published a half-century before *The Two Treatises of Civil Government*. In it he defended "the state of nature" as opposed to unlimited power of government: ". . . a state of perfect freedom" in which all men could "order their actions and dispose of their possessions and persons as they think fit, within the bounds of the law of nature, without asking leave or depending upon the will of any other man." The doctrine of inalienable rights was based on governmental authority kept in balance by *the consent of the governed*. Locke's implication is equality. "All men are by nature equal . . . every man enjoys the same rights that are granted to others."

The right of internal taxation belonged to Virginia, Wythe reasoned. For the crown to exercise that right it must have the colony's consent. In this case, Virginians would not consent.

This root of defiance would lead to a revolutionary document. The English view that American consent was implicit in alle-

giance to the king and that the colonists were *virtually* represented in Parliament, would be challenged repeatedly right up
until the final assertion, "Governments are instituted among
men, deriving their just powers from the consent of the governed."

If George Wythe kept a diary or Commonplace Book as was
customary, it did not survive the years. He rejected the idea of
writing an autobiography and may have prided himself on his
portentous memory to the extent that he refused to record his
reactions to daily events. We are the poorer. With detailed observations such as we find in the papers of Adams and Jefferson and
Franklin, to name the most familiar, it would be infinitely easier
to know the man.

However, the compatibility and devotion of Wythe and Jefferson for almost fifty years provides one of Wythe's soundest cha-
racterizations. From the mental and social habits formed by the
student after the example of his mentor, we have learned much
about the teacher.

Since he deplored anything smacking of superficiality, Wythe
pared down his intimate habits in order to have time and energy
for those interests contributing to learning. All of their lives, he
and Jefferson would greet the dawn with a cold shower, then
order the day so as to have plenty of reading time. Each preferred
books to people.

Their great friend Fauquier was a hard-drinking, profligate
gambler, far more typical of the successful, upper-class man of
the times. Wythe, moderate to an almost eccentric degree, set a
rather austere example for the protégé, Jefferson. But their absti-
nence is not as revealing perhaps as their tolerance for those with
lax habits. In their cellars, they stocked plentiful varieties of wine
and strong drink for guests with palates more sensual than their
own. They were not exclusive in their views, nor is there evidence that Wythe converted anyone else to his standards.

Yet, he was so radically democratic by the end of the Revolution that he objected to the aristocratic styles of powdered wigs
and the capitalizing of nouns. Even when writing in the first

person, for a while he used the lower case. Pupil Jefferson followed suit.

Among the wealthier traders and tobacco farmers, dandyism in wardrobe and ostentatious custom-made coaches and chaises were the same status symbols to which our modern affluent society has been addicted. Again, Wythe resisted trends. Not for him the bright damask coats and red morocco slippers of a John Hancock; his attire was conservative and simple although he indulged his vanity in quality cloth and flawless tailoring. Nor did he stint when it came to horses, and there is reason to think from orders to his London merchant that his saddle blankets were elegantly monogrammed and that he wanted his wife to be as stylish as the next one. No doubt such inconsistencies and quirks only made him more appealing to young Jefferson.

While Wythe required in his students a thorough knowledge of law, from ancient time through all the centuries to England's reformers, it seems he was equally intent on teaching Thomas Jefferson history, ethics, science, manners and hygiene, and literature with emphasis on poetry and plays. At a glance, this seems to be a rigorous program of study, even for the diligent Jefferson. So it was, but it is interesting that their relationship never took on the aspects of an apprenticeship, certainly not in the sense Wythe had served his uncle, Stephen Dewey. Instead, Wythe made assignments, then gave Jefferson freedom to pursue them in his own way, thus fostering a combination of originality and discrimination which would always set Jefferson apart.

In 1764, Dr. Small left Williamsburg for Birmingham, England, where he opened medical practice and continued his scientific experiments, took out patents on several inventions, and as an agent for the College of William and Mary, sent back the latest apparatus available. Wythe missed his friend Small, and since Jefferson was also deeply attached to his old math professor, the pursuit of the natural sciences in the student room at the Wythe house merely intensified to make up for their loss.

The following year, Thomas' favorite sister, Jane, died. Sensitive and moody, Jefferson felt deeply the absence of these two persons who had meant so much to him. Who could understand better than his tutor, George Wythe? He, too, had known loss at the deaths of Anne, the love of his youth, and of his stimulating, encouraging mother. Remembering afresh the kindness of Benjamin Waller who had fathered him through the torments of those desolate months, Wythe became Jefferson's emotional compass, leading the way out of mourning and setting the youth's course with hard work and study.

When Thomas left the capital to spend intervals with his family at Shadwell, Wythe assigned enough reading to keep the searching young mind engaged. Jefferson would write of himself, "I was bold in the pursuit of knowledge, never fearing to follow truth and reason to whatever results they led and bearding every authority which stood in the way."

Jefferson's teacher was in a large measure responsible for encouraging such intellectual vigor.

For the most part, Wythe's identity is so confined to the political system in which he operated that his Quaker background is all but obliterated; nevertheless, his instincts had been shaped by his mother's instruction and two generations of Quaker conscience. This, she and her son owed to the equal and independent intellectual status which Quakers allowed women.

Some very basic Quaker reforms coincided with those which engaged the mature Wythe. They were advanced concerns such as treatment of the insane, Indians, and Negroes; co-equal education; the inclusion of applied sciences in the college curriculum; religious liberty and separation of church and state; government with consent of the governed; political union in the colonies; freedom of thought and speech. These fundamentals can all be found in the writings of Penn, Bellers, and Woolman among other Quaker thinkers in the pre-Revolutionary era.

Wythe, of course, exposed his student "son," Jefferson, to these concepts through the broad reading assignments given the young man. And he and his teacher most probably discussed and debated these theories when Thomas was in the capital. Intellec-

The students' room or study in the Wythe House, restored as it looked when Wythe taught Jefferson. *Courtesy of the Colonial Williamsburg Foundation*

tual ferment must have charged the very air in that first floor back room of Wythe's home where his tutoring sessions were held.

The room has been restored, and in it one senses the variety of pursuits and compatible intimacy they shared. A round table with three chairs, a corner desk for reading, a tall one for writing, a bookcase, equipment including globes, telescopes, brass compass, barometer, slates for calculating, and so on. These objects were chosen to recreate the atmosphere and are not the original furnishings, but the simple stone fireplace unadorned by a man-

tel and the view of the garden from the windows opposite date
back to those days when this room was one of the most welcom-
ing the young Thomas Jefferson ever knew.

Was it there Wythe took him in order to congratulate him
privately upon being admitted in 1767 to the Bar of the General
Court, the highest in the colony? (The governor and council sat
with jurisdiction over both civil and criminal cases, but that
august body was not as learned as some of the advocates, notably
George Wythe, who had used his commanding position in behalf
of Jefferson.) Was it there, in the Wythe House student room, the
same year, that Jefferson spread out his first sketches of the site,
the terraces and orchards of Monticello? George and Elizabeth
Wythe would encourage the young man's dream of Monticello
and even provide him with grafts and cuttings from their own
prize specimens of horticulture. In such ordinary acts, Wythe
emphasized a diversity of values. A dynamic career was not the
sum of life. Rather, a basic harmony between man, his surroundings, and an expanding society, the integration of nature's form
with the mysteries of reason-developed wholeness, was the aim
of excellence.

VI

RIVALS AND REVERSALS

•

The Persuaders, Pendleton and Henry. Virginia's external threat of the Stamp Act and the internal raid on the treasury. Fauquier dies before the hospital for the insane can be started. Wythe becomes trustee of the hospital —the first of its kind in the colonies.

Truth and reason were the twin objectives paramount in George Wythe's legal teaching and practice, in his political career, and in his personal associations. This may account for the legendary detachment with which in later life he regarded cases from the bench. At the same time, this quality made him less effective in the role of advocate and most vulnerable in House debates with contemporaries Edmund Pendleton and Patrick Henry, two of his rivals with overpowering personalities.

Wythe and Jefferson, both ineffective speakers, considered themselves among the elite; yet they probably envied the colorful, crowd-swaying oratory of these skillful representatives. Outwardly, however, Wythe deprecated Pendleton's style, inferring that charm was not a substitute for sagacity. A curiously snobbish perversity in a champion of equality. Perhaps this was his reason for hesitating to sign Patrick Henry's license to practice law. Of course he was not the only one who thought Henry a fool from the backwoods of Louisa County, cheeky and preposterous to apply for a license after mere weeks of legal study. Wythe, a member of the royal governor's clique, Fauquier's foremost advisor in the colony, apparently underestimated Patrick Henry simply because he was a frontiersman. Unknown in the capital, easy-going, poor, and careless of dress, Henry was unimpressed by gentlemen aristocrats. His western people had been balky and discontented, particularly since a proclamation in 1763 forbade a British subject to buy or settle land west of the Allegheny ridge. Wythe knew that, but absorbed in his own lofty pursuits and the intricacies of the colony's power structure, he did not take serious notice of frontier causes, any more than he took Henry seriously. That is, not until the lawyer in his rough buckskins won instant fame in a case now known as the Parson's Cause. Henry, not yet thirty, really did not envy Justice Wythe his vast learning because Henry was a persuader of popular sentiment who with "torrents of sublime eloquence" (Jefferson's description) swayed both juries and his peers and, of course, his supporters, those westerners in the hill-'n'-holler country. The next thing Wythe knew, they had elected the upstart Henry to the House of Burgesses, and within a month he had become spokesman for those fellow members who represented the irrepressible freeholders on the Virginia frontier.

On an afternoon in May, 1765, "when the business of the Session was supposed to be over—except for the concluding ceremonies, and many of the Members retired of which I was one," recalled Edmund Pendleton, mighty leader of the Committee on Courts of Justice, "a letter was received from Mr. Montague the Agent inclosing a Copy of the Resolution of the Lords (or of the Commons agreed to by the Lords) for imposing Stamp duties. . . ."

All of the petitions written in forms of memorials drawn up by Wythe and his colleagues had been disregarded. "Without the consent" of the Virginians, or any other colonists, for that matter, the infamous Stamp Act had been forced upon all of the people without further debate.

Every will, deed, interrogatory, deposition, warrant, to name only a few of the documents necessary in legal dealings, must bear a royal stamp as ordered. Without compliance, the courts might as well close. Furthermore, the order applied to every bill of sale, bond, survey, contract, newspaper, newspaper ad, almanac, calendar, and pack of cards, even college degrees.

From the point of view of Britain's prime minister, George Grenville, and the Parliament, the stamp tax was a practical and equitable solution to the problem of getting the Americans together on the basic issue of defending themselves against another French campaign. Since each colony, occupied with local priorities, had reneged on the maintenance of adequate militia, a trained British army would be stationed in America at the colonists' expense. After all, they were British-Americans, and the people in England paid stamp taxes.

This seemed so logical to the government on the other side of the Atlantic that the House of Commons, asking few questions, had passed the Act 294 to 49.

But more than an ocean stretched between Grenville's expediency and American acceptance. The outcry was spontaneous and shrill up and down the Atlantic coast. In the Virginia House of Burgesses that May afternoon, with only thirty-nine members present (legislators haven't changed, not when the spring recess is due), Patrick Henry of Louisa County arose in the course of heated debate and with growing vehemence read to the House six resolutions. The last two, he and his supporters wrote, but the four preceding resolutions used exact passages from earlier resolves composed by Wythe.

Student Jefferson probably skipped afternoon studies to attend the House sessions because he was on hand that day, standing in the doorway, glancing around the room dominated by Speaker Robinson's high-backed chair, the associates' benches mostly empty ranging around the walls, and the clerk's table in the center.

Years later, according to his recollection of the occasion, Jefferson wrote that when Henry moved for his resolutions to be accepted the attorney general Peyton Randolph, Richard Bland, Pendleton, and Wythe jumped to their feet shouting, "Treason! Treason!" (In fact, Jefferson's recollection was a bit faulty. Pendleton was not present. The other three were.)

It is difficult to imagine such an emotional outburst from the restrained, orderly Wythe. "They did it not from any question of our rights," Jefferson explained, "but on the ground that the same sentiments had been, in their preceding session, expressed in a more conciliatory form, to which the answers were not yet received."

That "more conciliatory form" had been worked out following criticism of Wythe's original wording, called by some of his peers, also treasonable. Now here he was, using the same expletive! Not discounting a tender ego, Wythe was probably more alarmed by Henry's timing than by his plagiarism. The majority of the more-seasoned burgesses who had for years run Virginia's politics without challenge were not present to vote, and in that moment their power was transferred to Henry's generation. Henry and his backers rammed the resolution through (withholding the final ones they had prepared) after what Jefferson described as a "most bloody" debate, and after Henry, with cunning drama, apologized for affronting the speaker with his intemperate language. His apologies were about as sincere as his bows to the royal governor who, outraged, reported the incident to London, referring to Henry's young Turks as "hot and giddy." In effect, Fauquier's palace guard, particularly George Wythe, had been defied by an upstart from the hills. The governor's own authority was on the line; so Fauquier dissolved the House, minimizing Henry's victory. Elections would follow dissolution, and when word got around that the freshman lawyer from Louisa County had spoken audaciously of King George III, the governor believed Patrick Henry's chances for reelection would be slim.

Fauquier's reasoning proved how out of touch he was with frontier sentiment. Henry and his cronies were promptly returned to office. But so was Wythe, by the largest vote Elizabeth City County ever gave him. The royal governor suffered still another political loss with the death of the mighty John Robinson, speaker-treasurer. Far more than personal regret was involved; overnight the colony was rocked by scandal. The honorable, beloved treasurer had, without any authority whatever, passed a million dollars' worth of Virginia's currency among his aristocratic, debt-ridden friends, all from the most prominent families. Three notable exceptions—gentry who had *not* received large sums—were Washington, Peyton Randolph (a mere £10), and Wythe, who hoped to succeed Randolph as king's attorney.

Fauquier wanted, naturally, to appoint Wythe, and no one was more qualified than his friend and advisor. But the position was denied him because the late speaker and the Randolph brothers had formed a political machine even more powerful than Fauquier's. Robinson, who must have been as open-handed toward himself as toward his friends, had been a big land speculator (one grant alone, on the Greenbrier River, was for 100,000 acres). With the Randolphs he had formed the Loyal Land Company in competition with the Lee's Ohio Company. Robinson had succeeded their father, Sir John Randolph of Tazewell Hall, in the speaker's chair. Now Peyton took the late Robinson's place, and John took brother Peyton's. So continued another generation in the top offices by "hereditary" rights.

It goes without saying that when Richard Henry Lee pushed for full disclosure of embezzlement, the Randolph brothers along with other prominent dignitaries were incensed. They considered Lee a traitor to their kind. Lee joined up with Patrick Henry, no doubt because Henry had previously accused Robinson of underwriting "Spendthrifts." (Wythe would tell John Adams by way of explaining why Lee was ostracized by Virginia leaders at the Second Continental Congress that Lee "never recovered his reputation.")

The accepted habit of living beyond one's means and the equally accepted menace of an astronomical national debt are scarcely peculiar to our times. America started out that way, and the eighteenth-century Virginia oligarchy exemplifies today's spenders, dependent on credit to sustain the extravagances on which they were weaned.

During the unravelling of Robinson's heedless bookkeeping, other colonies were reacting to Patrick Henry's resolutions which had been published, including the last two, even though the Virginia House had not passed them. Readers of papers such as the *Massachusetts Gazette* and *Boston News-Letter* did not realize that, of course.

The "unofficial" resolves added up to inflammatory words around which popular resentment could rally: *Resolved, That the*

General Assembly of this Colony have the only and sole exclusive right and power to lay taxes and impositions upon the inhabitants of this Colony, and that every attempt to vest such power in any person or persons whatsoever other than the General Assembly aforesaid had a manifest tendency to destroy British as well as American freedom.

Resolved, That any person who shall, by speaking or writing, assert or maintain that any person or persons, other than the General Assembly of this colony, have any right or power to impose or lay any taxation on the people here, shall be deemed an enemy of His Majesty's colony.

School children know that mobs in Boston rioted, that they smashed the dock stamp office with axes, and hanged the stamp collector Andrew Oliver's effigy from what is now called the "Liberty Tree"; that in Connecticut, five hundred Sons of Liberty chased that colony's stamp collector, and when they caught him, forced him to resign. But do they know that when another of the king's stamp officers arrived in Williamsburg, Virginia, a different kind of mob, shouting "One and all!" went after him? Who knows what the man's fate would have been had not Fauquier taken him into the royal palace? This crowd, described in one of the governor's letters, was "chiefly . . . composed of Gentlemen of property in the Colony some of them at the Head of their respective Counties, and the Merchants of the Country. . . ."

As the fire of protest spread, Fauquier notified Parliament that "the Colonies reciprocally inflame each other and where the Fury will stop I know not." North, at Leedstown, four hundred "Friends of Liberty" descended upon a merchant in nearby Hobbs Hole who had said he would use the stamps. He speedily changed his mind.

Trade dwindled, the courts began closing; the colonies, on the edge of anarchy, were paralyzed, but so was England. The only practical thing to do was repeal the Stamp Act before it was really due to become enforced. Oddly enough, headlines announcing the repeal were preempted in the Virginia colony by notice of Speaker Robinson's death and the subsequent discovery that the Virginia treasury "had been robbed."

One crisis was displaced by the other; one imposed externally,

the other, internally. The entrenched Virginia leadership buck-
led under disgrace and ignominy. Although Wythe, like certain
other members of the House, should have known from the first
what was going on, he was appointed by the committee which
would examine the state of the treasury twice a year. Clearly, his
integrity had survived the Robinson debacle. Working closely
with the new treasurer, his old associate in law practice, Robert
Carter Nicholas, Wythe made himself indispensable on the ex-
amining committee. The historian, Dr. William Clarkin, points
out that even though George Wythe was no longer a member of
the House after the spring of 1768, the burgesses kept him on the
committee just the same—astonishingly irregular *and* compli-
mentary. He was indispensable to his colleagues, elected or not.
Furthermore, they swore him in as clerk of the House.

That spring was one of rapid change. Randolph's elevation to
the coveted position of attorney general was secondary compared
to the loss Wythe suffered upon the death of his great friend,
Francis Fauquier, who had sponsored him rather than Randolph
for the appointment. At sixty-five, the royal governor succumbed
to a "lingering illness and the feverest attacks of the most ex-
cruciating pain."

Among the more capable appointees by the crown to the
American colonies, Fauquier was mourned by Virginians, given
a ceremonial funeral at the Bruton Parish Church where he had
once sat under his silken canopy facing the paneled pulpit, refus-
ing to recite the Anglican creed. Was it omitted from the service
the day of his funeral? And did George Wythe supervise the
burial in the north aisle of the church? He was one of the four
executors of the royal governor's will.

In the face of spreading tensions, they had, together, kept the
colonial government uniform. In addition, the two friends had
collaborated on a most progressive *nonpolitical* plan for the "poor
unhappy set of People who are deprived of their Senses . . ."
reminding the Virginians that "Every Civilized country has an
Hospital for these People, where they are confined, maintained
and attended by able Physicians, to endeavor to restore them
their lost Reason."

Remember that the treatment of the mentally ill was often more inhuman than was the punishment of criminals during the eighteenth century. While the legislature was responsive to the royal governor's plan to care for the mentally ill, they did not act upon it until two years after his death, and still three more years would pass before the "lunatick Hospital" received patients. Wythe, one of the original trustees of this institution, the first of its kind in the colonies, helped make Fauquier's plan a reality at last—a fitting memorial to a benevolent, enlightened royal administrator.

VII

THE MIDDLE YEARS: 1769–1774

•

George Wythe, the mayor of Williamsburg and clerk of the House of Burgesses. George Wythe at home—husband, host, and friend.

The next five years, from 1769 to 1774, must have been among the most satisfying years Wythe knew. Still in his early forties, his reputation secure, he could fully utilize the experience gained from his terms in active representative politics.

At the same time, as clerk of the House, appointed solely on his merit, his involvement with the inner workings of government was assured while leaving him free to enlarge a gainful legal practice and to concentrate on still broader intellectual pursuits in the company of Jefferson who was now a burgess. The professor's pride in the young man's progress was more than that of a teacher; it was also parental.

And then there were during these years the social rewards of the highly cultivated art of Old Dominion hospitality. Elizabeth Wythe charmed their guests and delighted her husband. Described as "amiable in her disposition, engaging in her manners, and possessed of every virtue which could render her beloved," Elizabeth from the cultured line of Taliaferros enriched the climate of Wythe's social exposure. Even George's brilliance scarcely intimidated her, accustomed as she was to the peripatetic skills of her father, Richard Taliaferro, who had been popular in Williamsburg long before Wythe began a career there. In fact, Taliaferro, having been a justice, remained intimate with James City County politics and may have had a hand in the 1768 race for

Portrait of George Wythe as Chancellor of the High Court and professor of law. *Courtesy of the College of William and Mary, Earl Gregg Swem Library*

Williamsburg's mayor. In November of that year, his son-in-law was the winner—Mayor George Wythe.

The new mayor's home on Palace Street was already a landmark in Williamsburg illustrating Taliaferro's favorite hobby, whether or not his talent was original. English architectural books with specifications and plates were widely circulated in the colonies, and Batty Langley's *The City and Country Builder's and Workman's Treasury of Designs* may well have been in Taliaferro's library. Nevertheless, the Wythe House is proof that he understood classical scale, articulating an orderly instinct compatible with George Wythe's own.

A sure sense of this compatibility overcame me recently while looking once more into the study, a room at the rear of the first floor on the left side of the hall. Here was Wythe's retreat. By closing the door, he could remain undisturbed in peaceful privacy. Against whitewashed walls, the slate blue of window frames and recessed shutters was a color somehow agreeable to him, a color that melded into the sky beyond. My thoughts drifted back in time to another summer day when Wythe had sat at the desk in this room observing a similar scene. Moments before, the sunshine seemed to shrivel the ovals of lavender and thyme, mint and rue in the side garden. Then, as he watched, a small cloud passed over, trailing a generous shower. Older Tidewater folk still compared such a sudden blessing to "the sweetness of Elizabeth our virgin queen," for whom the colony had been named. Virginia. The sky, mirrored in the round multi-paned chancel window in the church next door, even touched the bricks capping the churchyard wall with azure. Only the new steeple was limned by a westering sun.

I could see Wythe, a shy smile on his face, fixing his attention once more upon the letter before him. It was addressed to his cousin Courtney Walker's husband, John Norton, Eq., of the prominent mercantile firm in London. From the numerous orders Wythe sent Norton during this period we can infer that the gentleman must have had great knowledge of Wythe's affairs, that Norton knew firsthand the details of his client's finances. He knew Chesterville's crop potentials, whether or not enough tobacco was produced to finance the fastidious tastes of George and Elizabeth. Besides, there was the flowering law practice, enriched by the advantages of position—George Wythe, clerk of the House of Burgesses, practitioner before the General Court, mayor of Williamsburg. On the basis of all this, Norton extended limitless credit, apparently free of risk.

From ads appearing in the *Virginia Gazette*, a reader wonders if many of the items Wythe ordered were not imported to the colony and available right in Williamsburg shops. Perhaps the gentry considered local merchandise inferior. In Wythe's case, he may have sought to keep his business to himself. One exception was the account he kept with his barber and wigmaker on the Duke of Gloucester Street across from the Raleigh Tavern.

Norton, undoubtedly a factor for several wholesale outlets, could, of course, provide the astonishing variety of goods the Wythes preferred, ranging from professional paraphernalia for George to a fashionable wardrobe for Elizabeth.

Lists of these purchases suggest the status of the enviable couple in the gracious house facing onto the Palace Green: complete services of fine china and crystal, linen for sheets, damask for tablecloths (huckaback was the "daily" material used when guests were not present), blanket and quilt yardage and shoes for the servants, a bonnet for Mrs. Wythe, velvet breeches, silk waistcoats and stockings for the master, "a well built handsome postcharriott," and books, always books. Wythe was constantly adding to his personal library and to the library he was collecting in the House of Burgesses. Thus he placed orders for engraved bookplates.

As Clerk, he needed the journals of the House of Commons proceedings from which he may have decided upon a style for his own minutes, copied meticulously into the new volumes Norton supplied.

Wythe also needed large stocks of parchment for his office and adopted certain refinements from the English Parliament such as balloting glasses, an "inkstand fit for public office," and a robe of quality. He called the one he had worn "scandalous."

The pipes of madeira and carboys of arrack ordered for the

Bookplate. *Reproduced through the courtesy of the Virginia Historical Society*

Wythes' cellar suggest elaborate entertainment since the host himself was all but an abstainer.

Most of these items, along with a "Gentleman's saddle" and a blue horsecloth ornamented—the new chariot must also be adorned with a coat-of-arms of Wythe's design—reveal quite a few aristocratic inclinations in a man who refused to capitalize the *S* in the noble title *Sir*.

When Fauquier's successor, Norborne Berkeley, Baron de Botetourt, sailed into Hampton Roads aboard the H.M.S. *Rippon*, crowds of loyal Virginians prepared an official welcome in the capital. The whole town of Williamsburg was "illuminated" by candles and torches and fireworks; a holiday mood enveloped new Governor Botetourt and his people. Wythe resumed the role of advisor to the king's man, in spite of the fact that by this time he was a person with vast influence at the very hub of Virginia's resistance to that king. This resistance was fired by the invidious Townshend duties which had been slapped on basic commodities by a divided Parliament caught up in controversy over colonial taxation. None of these articles—glass, paint, lead, paper, tea—taxed by the new act, appeared in Wythe's orders. Because these imports were boycotted by the angry Americans, the act failed to produce expected revenue. Furthermore, the House had sent (as in the case of the Stamp Act) another petition to the home government which was considered by that body to be impudent. Botetourt had his instructions which were based on England's determination to "reject as null and void, every Act and Proceeding in Our Colonies, inconsistent with and derogatory from Our said Right (to enact laws without consent), and that We do therefore highly disapprove their said Petition to Us."

The new, amiable governor consulted with all leaders in the Virginia Assembly and persuaded them "to return to a becoming Sense of their Duty, founded upon just Ideas of the Constitution." Surely the old members "by their great steadiness and moderation" would control the young hotheads in restoring a "pacific temper."

On Monday, May 8, 1769, Botetourt presided over his first meeting of the Assembly without a ripple of hostility. Gregarious and unaffected, his very presence reassured George Wythe who soon entertained the royal governor informally. Wythe, the host, put every guest, regardless of social position, at ease.

The guest list was not limited to persons of distinction. On the contrary, students from the College of William and Mary freely drifted in and out for meals and discussions. Off and on, a student would stay at the Wythe home while studying with the distinguished pedagogue. And, lest this suggest a rarefied classroom atmosphere, it is well to add that Elizabeth's brother, Richard Taliaferro II and his wife, the former Rebecca Cocke, had at least seven children, who often visited.

Reportedly, children found George Wythe irresistible. During those peaceful middle years, he enjoyed the mischief and laughter of the young Taliaferros. If they, with their parents and grandparents, arrived from nearby Powhatan, a minimum of thirteen were seated around the table, noisy and festive. This must have been a special joy for the childless Elizabeth and George.

The Wythes traveled to the peninsula to consult with the overseer of Chesterville and possibly arranged for George's sister and her family to come over from Norfolk for brief reunions. There may have been a particular fondness for her grandson if one significant fact is taken into account: Wythe would, in his old age, draw a will leaving the bulk of his estate to his sister's grandson, his namesake, George Wythe Sweney. (For a time Wythe even shared his home with the boy.)

Always, Wythe was surrounded by youthful students, a sure sign that he remained as entertaining as he was provocative. In other words, here was a man at home with young people, with his peers, royal governors and presidents, and with foreign celebrities. (Comte de Rochambeau, like Washington, would use the Wythe house for quarters.) As Oscar L. Shewmake's popular quote expresses it, "George Wythe, Gentleman, the trusted and beloved friend of presidents and ministers of state, stray dogs and little children."

This warm, generous side of George Wythe has been almost obscured by the volume of documents and formal correspondence reflecting his legal erudition, ornamented by obscure but favorite Greek and Latin phrases, and, in some politicians' opinions, an attitude of distinct superiority.

But one cannot read his note to Sam Adams, beginning "how d'ye?" with references to their first collaboration at an early Congress in Philadelphia and miss the nosy, nostalgic mood of Wythe as he wrote the letter. "Tell me what more you would say if we were eating a saturday's dinner at mrs. Yard's, smoking a pipe in the political club at the Indian queen—holding a tete a tete at my apartment opposite to Israel's gardens—or rambling towards Kensington. In a word, anything, news, or what you please will be gratefully rec'vd."

Nor can one miss the warmth of concern in a favorite of mine from all of Wythe's letters. It was sent to Jefferson at his new home place after Shadwell, the Jefferson family home, had burned to the ground. Thomas then moved into a one-room structure built on a nearby mountain he had roamed as a child. There he could isolate himself with nature and work at clearing the mountaintop for Monticello. He plunged into landscaping and the establishment of an orchard. The letter from his teacher must have moved the sensitive young dreamer with needed encouragement and tender emotion. Who knew more about orchards than friend Wythe who enlarged his own at Chesterville upon acquiring Syms' two hundred acres of fruit trees which he had finally planted at Chesterville? (Generations before, the will of the first Thomas Wythe specified, "I give unto my Loveing Sonn Thomas Wythe three Negroes by Name Tom, Rose, Robin and all my Land and halfe the p'duce of the Orchards he finding help to beate the Sider.")

G.W. to T.Jefferson.

I send you some nectarine and apricot grafts and grape vines, the best I had; and have directed your messenger to call upon major Taliaferro for some of his. You will also receive two of Foulis's catalogues. Mrs. Wythe will send you some garden peas.

You bear your misfortunes so becomingly that, as I am convinced you will surmount the Difficulties it has plunged you into, so I foresee you will hereafter reap advantages from it several ways. *Durate, te vosmet rebus servate secundis.*

9 Mar 1770

Undoubtedly Wythe felt most deeply about the loss of Jefferson's carefully acquired library and personal papers in the Shadwell fire, but until another library could be collected, there was the therapy of work blessedly close to the earth. There were seeds to plant, trees and grapevines to mulch. Out of the soil, a mystical source of growth, came everything. Jefferson and Wythe were bound together by a law transcending statesmanship—conserving while utilizing nature's wealth. This law George Wythe had learned firsthand and with humility.

VIII

CONFRONTATION

•

Virginia's first secret Association convened. The ambitious earl of Dunmore becomes royal governor. Boston's tea party and blockade. Virginia supports the "common cause." First Continental Congress.

While these busy years were fulfilling for George Wythe, the poorer classes in the colony suffered a variety of plagues ranging from smallpox epidemics to "a prodigious hail" which damaged the '68 crops, broke windows, and killed sheep. The hail may have accompanied a tornado since there was "a violent gust of wind" leaving behind uprooted trees and demolished chimneys.

From a reading of the *Gazette*, we learn these facts plus the fact that circulation of that tabloid obviously depended more on advertisers than on local reporting. Wythe ordered kitchen garden seeds from Norton, but long lists were imported by the capital merchant, William Wills, for sale: The variety of "Pease" for instance included Early garden hotspur; Spanish marrotes; Bunch; Sugar blues; Dutch Admiral; Early Lisbon; Long kids; White blossoms. Most European countries exported specialties, judging from the seed lists: "Russian cabbage; Italian celery; Silesia lettuce. Colliflower and broccoli and cucumbers and parsnips and turnips and spinage and corn and betes and endive and onions and narsturtiums" were available at Wills' shop.

"By permission of the Worshipful Mayor of Williamsburg" the Virginia Company of Comedians came to town and performed a tragedy, *Venice Preserved* or *A Plot Discovered,* and a ballad opera, *Damon and Phillida.* Mr. Russell sold tickets from his store next to the post office. At this particular performance, "No person whatever" would be admitted backstage. Ladies reserving boxes were advised to send their servants early in advance of a performance. That seemed the only sure way of holding their seats until curtain time.

If music was "the favorite passion of Jefferson's soul," theater and dancing and racing were George Washington's enthusiasms. Whether or not he saw *Venice Discovered* is not recorded, but we do know that when he came to Williamsburg for these diversions, he frequently stopped by the Wythes for luncheon. The fashionable six-foot two-inch planter, striking in the saddle, rode up to the house after a four-day journey from Mt. Vernon. He was greeted by a groom who appreciated Squire Washington's superb thoroughbred and by Elizabeth and George who eagerly exchanged news before their friend went on to the popular racing track at Williamsburg where gentlemen brought their fastest horses during the season. (They were the only ones allowed the luxury of the sport. "Laborers" were shut out by law.)

Besides betting at the track, they gambled on cockfights, at cards, or on most any game, "putt," or "hazard." Gambling at the Raleigh Tavern was even more in favor than dancing, but dancing and music were great entertainments at house parties. Naturally it was an asset for any black servant to sing and play instruments. Some were in demand for their talents. In the capital, sarabands, gavottes, minuets, and the Virginia reel were taught by dancing masters. Legend has it that one ball given by Richard Lee lasted six days. The guests went home exhausted.

Royalists may have picked up the tune their kind were singing in Boston, ridiculing the early would-be patriots: *Come, Shake Your Dull Noddles, ye pumpkins, and bawl, And own that you're mad at fair Liberty's call* ... Liberty was not yet an issue in the Virginia colony.

Between acts at the theater, Master Peter Pelham conducted a small chamber group. Everyone knew him. He had helped install the Bruton Parish Church organ and then played it for fifty years, although for the first eighteen he received no salary. He taught music as did Francis Russworm. One of the Carters had his own organ along with other instruments. And one of Franklin's many inventions was the "Armonica." Such a pleasure-loving society might be expected to neglect church obligations. Not at all. Mr. Pelham's choir was well trained, and the well-known music instructor, Fithian, accustomed to hearing "the Clerk & about two others" make up the congregational singing in his New Jersey hometown, was much impressed by the psalm- and hymn-singing in Virginia. Everyone participated and was trained in what he judged a "respectable Method."

The love of music was an important tie between Wythe and young Jefferson. Jefferson bought himself a "good" violin in 1768. It is appropriate that in the restored Wythe House a piano fills a corner of the parlor. A mandolin has been added, and a fife or German flute rests on the Chippendale music stand.

The mayor of Williamsburg possibly dealt with an outbreak of rabies since the *Gazette* suggested this *Recipe for the Bite of a Mad Dog*: "Take of the leaves of rue picked from the stalks and bruised, 6 oz. Garlick, picked clean and bruised, 6 oz. Venice treacle or Mithridate and scrapings of pewter, of each 4 oz."

Apparently the prescription was both for the victim and for the dog because instructions were: "Boil all over a slow fire in two quarts of strong ale, until the pint is consumed. Strain it and keep it in a bottle close stopped, and give of it nine spoonfuls warm to the person seven mornings successively. Six spoonfuls will cure a dog, and nine days after the bite, apply some of the ingredients to the wound."

It is unlikely that George Wythe overlooked anything in a newspaper, especially the recaps of English history, used by the *Virginia Gazette* editor to fill space. This one appeared in the February 1768 issue featuring a colorful quote by Cromwell, one of the past's most powerful lord protectorates.

Ye are a pack of mercenary wretches, and would, like Esau, sell your country for a mess of pottage; and, like Judas, betray your God for a few pieces of money. Is there a single virtue now remaining amongst you? Is there one vice ye do not possess? Ye have no more religion than my horse. Gold is your god. Which of you has not bartered your consciences for bribes? Is there a man amongst you that hath the least care for the good of the Commonwealth? Ye sordid prostitutes!

Wythe would have known the occasion for that rhetoric well indeed. In 1655 Cromwell had dissolved Parliament after the members voted that his office must be elective. (Lawyers in Virginia probably still quoted Cromwell whenever it served their purpose.) That had been over one hundred years ago. Rereading it in seemingly uneventful times may have been amusing, but some events have a way of repeating—and the recognizable repetition shocks us into sobriety.

When Governor Botetourt, in fewer and far more moderate words, exercised Cromwellian authority by dissolving the House of Burgesses in 1769, Wythe and the legislators were not at all amused. The almost euphoric rapport between Virginians and their royal governor was shattered in a matter of hours by a calamitous maneuver in which Wythe, the clerk of the House, played a role.

Beloved as Fauquier had been, the Baron de Botetourt evidently evoked an ever deeper affection from Virginians. In no way did he resemble the image most commoners had of nobility; his open face was homely; his figure, short and rugged which only made him seem more approachable. Gentle as Androcles, the royal governor Botetourt's interest in "the humblest visitor in social circles" endeared him to all the people.

Wythe and the governor were closely associated, of course, privately and in the business of the colony. Clerk of the House Wythe was ranked higher than the one position might suggest, as is indicated by his important appointment to the board of William and Mary College—Visitor Wythe, Vestryman Wythe, Mayor Wythe, Clerk of the Burgesses Wythe. His law practice excelled, and with three of the most powerful men in the government, Robert Carter Nicolas, Peyton Randolph, and John Randolph, he had completed the collation of the laws of the colony —a four-year job. His involvement with hospital plans for the insane continued, and at last he was about to get underway the construction of a much needed courthouse.

Whatever Botetourt needed to know, Wythe was at his elbow ready with information and counsel. Inevitably, their loyalties conflicted, however, when Parliament added to the odious Townshend duties a cunning but unwise demand that anyone caught smuggling forbidden items must be taken to England for trial. From that country's point of view the reason was simply that a colonial jury never convicted smugglers of tea or any of the other Townshend articles because the jury consisted of consumers. But the removal of any American to a court in England for whatever reason insulted the colonists' sense of pride in their capacity for justice.

The House of Burgesses decided to toss this incendiary bomb back to its inventors. A resolution was drawn rejecting the act as "highly derogatory of the rights of British subjects."

Botetourt knew he would be blamed for the Virginia resistance and tried to head it off. First, he sent a messenger for a copy of the minutes from which he could study the debate leading up to the resolve. The poor fellow was sent away empty-handed, only to be sent back again the next morning by the governor. The doors of the House chambers were locked. Inside, the wording was agreed upon, and Wythe had the minutes entered in the House journals; only then were the doors unlocked and the resolution taken to the governor waiting in the council chamber. Annoyed by the delaying tactics, Botetourt studied it carefully. His final opinion was that the burgesses had gone too far in their protest, leaving him only one option. Without ceremony, Governor Botetourt dissolved the session.

For the first time (it would not be the last), Virginia's leaders ignored the crown's representative and reassembled in the home of Anthony Hay to form an "Association." Moderator Peyton Randolph helped a committee draft an agreement to boycott the importation of all items listed in the hated Townshend Act, and by the fall meeting of the Assembly six months later, Botetourt announced that the duties would be lifted (except on tea, significantly). The victory must have been a bit heady for the protesters. Hadn't they already forced the repeal of the Stamp Act? Now

Britain had backed down again.

In spite of the growing obstructionism, some idea of the still unruffled amicable association between the colonists and their governor emerges from the accounts of Christmas celebrations in Williamsburg that year. When the House of Burgesses recessed for the holidays, they gave an elegant ball for Botetourt. Yet it should be noted that the most fashionable ladies of the capital society wore "Virginia cloth" woven on their own looms to remind him of the boycott against English goods.

The next session in May 1770 was orderly enough when it opened, but the Non-Importation Association soon put on the pressure for everyone to join them. Not all colonies had entered into the boycott and some burgesses even favored amendment of it. Again, with Peyton Randolph leading, the associates trooped out of their chamber in the capitol to the nearby Raleigh Tavern. They began a round of seventeen toasts to the king, ending,

> *May the Rose flourish,*
> *The Thistle grow,*
> *And the Harp be tuned*
> *To the cause of American liberty.*

The cause of American liberty was more than a toast; it was a revolt against external authority which was gaining impetus.

It was not a good year for Virginia. Floods wiped out crops, bringing on further depression, and in October, Lord Botetourt died. Material misfortunes did not compare with the loss of His Excellency, a fair and good-natured ruler. The citizens mourned him because they honestly esteemed and loved him. There would not be another royal governor of whom that could be written. The confrontation between Botetourt's successor and the Assembly would propel Virginia toward independence.

Again, George Wythe was made one of the executors of a deceased governor's estate. By then no lawyer surpassed his reputation for sagacity and justice. It was well known that if he discovered a client was being untruthful with him, he returned the fee and let someone else have the case. This is not to say that he was without rivals, the most celebrated being Edmund Pendleton from Virginia's Caroline County. The two had first met in the Caroline court during Wythe's circuit-riding years. Pendleton was already established then (Wythe was five years younger) and had preceded to the General Court ahead of Wythe. Elected a burgess in 1752, Pendleton would serve without interruption until 1774.

Both men worked tirelessly; both gave scrupulous attention to details. Without formal education both developed their practice of the law successfully—Wythe drawn to classical studies, Pendleton content with practical knowledge. The latter preferred a "spicy best-seller" (*Tristram Shandy*) and collections of hell-and-brimstone sermons. Wythe's taste ran to Erasmus' *Adages* and the writings of Euripedes, in Greek, of course.

Their most quoted observer, Hugh Blair Grigsby, drew the contrast between the two lawyers this way: "Pendleton was strictly a man of talents, and regarded all knowledge merely as a means of pursuing his ends with success. Wythe was a man of genius, and loved knowledge for its own sake."

In other words, Wythe was the scholar. But that in no way made up for the more appealing personality of Pendleton, who was handsome, gregarious, confident, and, most significantly, a masterful orator.

Exact in diction, intense in the presentation of a case, Wythe must have been often indignant—even puzzled—when time and again Pendleton won with seeming ease. Wythe was more frustrated than puzzled probably, judging from an account written years later by Henry Clay who, as a young man, was Wythe's secretary: "On one occasion, when Mr. Wythe, being opposed to Mr. Pendleton, lost the case, in a moment of vexation declared . . . that he would quit the bar, go home, take orders, and enter the pulpit." The friend to whom Wythe said this thought it a poor solution since Pendleton might do the same, and in the pulpit, as at the bar, "beat you there."

Pendleton, aware of his compelling eloquence, may have relished the competition, while Wythe, contemptuous of the end-justifies-the-means school, felt his defeats were synonymous with

Portrait of Edmund Pendleton. *Courtesy of the Virginia State Library.*

the miscarriage of justice. However, it would seem that their differences were mainly those of personality and superficial jealousy since the two stars of the General Court, the highest in the colony, eventually cooperated in parliamentary maneuvers in order that Patrick Henry might be defeated.

One thing is certain: There was nothing superficial about the animosity Wythe came to feel toward the new governor appointed after Botetourt's death—John Murray, the fourth earl of Dunmore. An oft-related story is used to prove this point: The "very pretty, smooth-tongued" Pendleton and an associate were scheduled to debate a case before Dunmore who presided over the General Court. Their opponents were Wythe and Robert Carter Nicholas. When Pendleton's associate did not show up on time, Pendleton asked the governor to delay the proceedings. To which Dunmore is said to have replied, "Go on, Mr. Pendleton. You'll be a match for both of them." Wythe and Nicholas reddened with anger. Bowing low, in order to accentuate the mockery of his words, Wythe responded, ". . . with your Lordship's assistance." To observers, the courtly gesture was clearly condescending. It was Dunmore's turn to blush. The story seems to support claims that this governor lacked diplomatic tact and that it was not the only time that Mr. Wythe's gray eyes regarded Dunmore with scorn.

A Scottish peer, the earl of Dunmore, had been transferred from New York, where he had acquired 51,000 acres of land, to Virginia, where he became a favorite of the large land speculators. (Lord Fairfax, for one, gave him 3,465 acres.) Never a member of that inner fraternity of great landholders, Wythe must have looked upon the governor as a mere opportunist. Virginia's territorial grants westward were guarded by Wythe, but he never personally contracted "land fever."

The first time Dunmore presided over the Assembly, after postponing three sessions (roads were impassable the winter of 1771), he was the victim of assorted crises, the worsening economy spawning most of them. The English Board of Trade which regarded the colonies as simply suppliers of natural goods depended on a triangle of exchange. Molasses was shipped from the

West Indies to New England where it was used to produce rum. Then rum went to Africa for slaves. The slaves whom the rum bought were in turn brought to the colonies and sold. Slaves were rightly called the "lifeblood of empire." Virginia, its agriculture dependent upon slave labor, had traded and sold Indians from the birth of the colony. By the middle 1700s Negroes ranked even lower than Indians on the social scale. They were "real estate," figured literally into a man's worth . . . "Chattels . . . considered no otherwise than Horses or Cattle, And there is no doubt but the Increase of any living Creature after the deathe of the Testor, are looked upon as part of his Estate, and are liable to be taken for his Debts."

It is paradoxical that both George Wythe and Jefferson benefited from this perfectly legal provision, while repeatedly testing it in the courts. In fact, during his first term in the House of Burgesses, Jefferson audaciously drew a bill giving slaveholders the choice of freeing their slaves. Richard Bland, senior member, put forward the legislation in Jefferson's behalf and was predictably dubbed a traitor by the colony's planters. It would not be Jefferson's only defeat on the issue.

At this early stage in his political career, Jefferson was still intellectually influenced by Wythe. Certainly they echoed each other in espousing the liberation of American decisions from the absolute power of the English. Emancipation was just one cause tied into their larger concepts of equality, religious liberty, free co-education, and the controversial union of the colonies.

It may be coincidence that these were fundamentals of Quaker theory evident in William Penn's "Holy Experiment," but when George Keith, Wythe's great-grandfather had taught alongside Penn, he was known on both sides of the Atlantic for his antislavery views. The mighty Scot, pamphleteer and preacher, was quoted (by Benjamin Franklin, as noted previously) on the subject even after he switched to Anglican missions.

In 1671, George Fox had denounced slavery upon visiting Barbadoes. In 1688 the Quakers of Germantown, Pennsylvania, had followed his lead. In 1711 Pennsylvania's Quaker Assembly had their law against slave importation vetoed by the Crown.

Freedom of whites, blacks, Indians, women, children, regardless of class, was the broader objective. And in the Declaration
the definition of equality is enlightened by Quaker thought: "It
means equality of respect and the resulting absence of all words
and behavior based on class, racial or social distinctions," according to the modern authority, Howard Brinton, who adds, "It did
not, for example, place on an economic equality employer and
employee or master and servant." Even so, within the frame of
the period, the concept was progressive and at odds with the
interests of England's most powerful corporation, the East India
Company, which controlled the wealth produced by colonial
trade. Dunmore, who would later turn the slavery issue into a
recruiting tactic, ignored Jefferson's ideas about manumission, as
did the Virginia Assembly, and concentrated instead on the vast
potential of expanding westward. Having invested in Washington's land company, Dunmore's motive was personal *and* served
the military interest of his government.

Wythe, on the other hand, was about the business of two projects which reflected his own intimate enthusiasms. He began
tutoring another brilliant student, St. George Tucker, and he
helped launch the Society for the Promotion of Useful Knowledge, an outlet for yet another cause—science. Both undertakings
rounded out his active life in Williamsburg. But that small town
was far removed from the port cities of Philadelphia, Charleston,
New York, and Boston. In Boston, according to Abigail Adams'
words, a "flame is kindled and like lightning it catches from Soul
to Soul." Boston's Tea Party remains the best publicized of several along the eastern seaboard, its meaning either exaggerated or
belittled. In perspective, the event underscores the shrewdness of
the colonists and the degree to which that shrewdness was underestimated by the British. The royal government, having agreed
more or less to bail out the great East India Company for its
surpluses of stale tea, allowed the tea to be shipped directly to the
Americans at a reduced price. They were certain that the bargain
would be irresistible in the colonies, that the company's losses
would soon be recouped, and, of course, that the royal government would collect taxes. Instead, the tea never reached the colo-

nists' docks: they could manage without British patronage!

Boston was not the only place where the tea was tossed rashly to the tide, but Boston was singled out by the crown for an example of the punishment which such uncouth, defiant acts deserved. The port of Boston was blockaded. The message seemed to be that if Americans would not buy tea—"that baneful weed"—then they would buy nothing else. Furthermore, dependent upon waterways for all commerce, Americans could not accept goods from another country: "Be it enacted, that no vessel, lighter, boat or bottom, no goods, wares or merchandise whatever. . . ." The foolish dictum implied, drink tea or starve.

Faneuil Hall was soon crowded with patriots who first petitioned the Almighty to help them. Then, drawing up their own version of the Boston Port Bill, they dispatched copies to the other colonies. In the face of all this sparring, Jefferson, with other burgesses, "cooked up a resolution," calling for a day of public prayer. Virginia joined Boston's protest. From Norfolk, the colony's most exposed port, a message went north to Massachusetts declaring, ". . . we consider you as suffering in the common cause and look upon ourselves as bound by the most sacred ties to support you."

This time it was Dunmore who dissolved the Virginia House. Again, the members trooped over to Raleigh Tavern. Again, they chose Peyton Randolph to lead them. This time it was decided that a congress of all colonies be called. In fact, they proposed an annual congress of appointed deputies from each colony. The punishment of Boston had triggered unprecedented union; it was plain that what had happened in one colony could happen to the others; their interests were interlocked. If troops were pouring into Boston to bring submission to the authority of King George III, troops could be sent to other ports as well.

Colonel Washington, who had often visited with Dunmore at his country place, Porto Bello (five miles east of Williamsburg), in order to discuss their land speculations, now reacted with uncharacteristic impetuosity. He would, he declared, draft 1,000 soldiers, pay them out of pocket, lead them up to Boston, and confront England's Lieutenant General Thomas Gage! If the king—British America's king—resorted to force, so would his colonists.

We know, of course, that Washington did not go to Boston that summer. Instead, he went home for several weeks, supervised the building of an addition at Mt. Vernon, then returned to Williamsburg for the August session of the House. Before the month was over he, with six other delegates, was in Philadelphia for the First Continental Congress.

The members of the House remaining in session in Williamsburg included George Wythe and Thomas Jefferson. The two men agreed once and for all that an English Parliament had no business interfering with Virginia's trade and internal government and that Virginia's status was comparable to Scotland's, independent though giving allegiance to the king. Jefferson sent instructions spelling out this distinction to the delegates in Philadelphia who found the idea far too inflammatory, as did his conservative colleagues in Williamsburg. Contrary to what some writers claim, Wythe was not all that cautious because Thomas Jefferson later wrote, "In this doctrine . . . I had never been able to get anyone to agree with me but Mr. Wythe." The two friends had reasoned together and reached the same conclusion. From that moment Wythe was recognized by the forward men of the colonies as a radical on the issue of American self-government.

If the earl of Dunmore knew about the meeting of delegates in Williamsburg's best tavern and in the Philadelphia Congress, it did not deter him from a military campaign which history would label Dunmore's War. The governor shucked the quarrel with his unruly legislators and prepared for the kind of action he relished. It must have been a relief to get away from the sultry confines of the Virginia capital. Soldiers understood him. He was at home with them. From the fort sharing his name in Pittsburgh, Lord Dunmore, jaunty in his tam'o'shanter, led twelve hundred troops down the Kanawha Valley, where eventually he was joined by Andrew Lewis's men, and at Point Pleasant (located near Charleston, West Virginia) defeated the Shawnee Indians, negotiated with them a treaty favorable to the British, and returned triumphantly to his palace in Williamsburg.

When the royal governor called the Assembly into session the fall of 1774, his mind was probably more on the frontier than on the agenda at hand. However, he must have known that trouble was brewing, judging by the orders he had received from His Majesty King George III by way of Lord Dartmouth, secretary of state to the colonies. The orders were that Dunmore, along with the other colonial governors, must make certain that all arms and ammunitions supplied Virginia's militia remain under his control. The governor eagerly plotted a stratagem which he considered failproof. From a military standpoint it was, but he miscalculated the emotional temper of the Virginians. He would pay for his miscalculation in more ways than one.

XI

THE FLAME IS KINDLED

•

Dunmore's miscalculation. "First shot" begins the Revolution. Wythe joins protest march. Replaces Commander-in-Chief Washington in the Continental Congress.

The First Continental Congress was a warning that Parliament simply could not disregard. If the colonies stuck to their new nonimportation resolves, the discipline England had meted out to those "children planted by our care" had clearly backfired. Franklin wrote from London, encouraging Americans in the boycott. From his vantage point he was certain that if it lasted long enough, the accumulation of insults would be redressed, the colonial rights "acknowledged . . . and the aggrieving Laws be repeal'd." Until this time, working for reconciliation, the Pennsylvanian had been a friendly diplomat, but the Boston Port Bill had changed all that. He now shared the desperation and rage of his friends in the Congress and delighted in the surprise their unanimity had handed Britain.

Parliament was surprised, but the royal governors in the colonies were more than surprised—they felt threatened. Dunmore must have grasped the whole picture upon realizing that the speaker of the Virginia Assembly also led the Congressional delegates. He knew little of the proceedings, however. To keep the deliberations of Congress secret, the doors of Carpenter Hall were always locked during sessions.

The governor, trying to serve the best interests of the colony and his king, adjourned the Assembly. The action would have no more effect than on the previous occasion; the legislators knew full well that they could convene at a place and time of their own choosing.

By Christmas, the counties through Committees of Safety kept tab on all merchants. If one sidestepped the nonimportation resolve and obtained English goods, he was exposed so that the public could punish him by boycotting the shop. In Williamsburg, George Wythe was elected to the local committee of safety. (The other three members were Speaker Randolph, Benjamin Waller, and associate Robert Carter Nicholas.) Whenever ethical, impartial judgments were required, Wythe's appointment was automatic. What with the leading citizens of the capital "enforcing" patriotic compliance, it may have been a dull winter. The courts were scarcely functioning, shopkeepers watched their shelves empty, and the spring session of the House which always brought members and their families from every corner of the colony was in doubt.

Even though Williamsburg was still quiet that March, it was decided that Richmond was a safer meeting place for the burgesses—far enough removed from the royal governor's spying. The secret session was attended by chosen representatives, and their decisions revolved around one central issue—the defense of the colony. This was proof that tension between America and the mother country was accelerating. The hard choice between a permanent army and a beefing-up of each county's volunteer militia proves that the once unthought-of confrontation was by this time anticipated.

At this Richmond convention Patrick Henry made his most quoted battle cry, "I know not what course others may take, but as for me, give me liberty, or give me death!" Preceding the fiery slogan, he declared that the war was already begun in the north. There would be no escape for Virginia.

Henry's eloquence apparently persuaded the delegates to his view; he favored a militia rather than a full-time army and his reasoning was sound. The small land owners whom he had rallied into a political force could not afford to be away from their farms, and since their numbers were swelling with the westward push, a militia was the cheapest and most practicable solution. With realistic foresight, Washington was among those chosen to attend the next session of the Continental Congress coming up. Having been the only aide to survive the humiliating defeat at Fort Necessity, he was already something of a hero, and his experience in the French-Indian War qualified him for military leadership if events reached the point of no return.

Within a month that is exactly what happened in Virginia and in New England. Dunmore, correctly reading the meaning of a covert militia in his colony, knew he dared not wait another moment to carry out Lord Dartmouth's orders. An armed English ship was conveniently moored just southwest of the capital (the inlets of the James and those of the York River, almost equidistant from his country place, were ideal avenues of escape), and the governor needed the ship. Under cover of night, he brought off enough marines to raid Williamsburg's octagonal, solid brick powder magazine.

Even though the marines worked "privately," they were discovered. Throughout the sleeping town, alarm was hissed person to person, door to door; militiamen signaled with drums, bells tolled. Though George Wythe was not in the militia, he probably hurried, more erect and energetic than ever, around the corner to Market Square, where the magazine stood on the south side of the main street opposite *his* courthouse. The arms and ammunition were gone.

Abigail Adams' phrase, "the flame is kindled," was now as true in Virginia as in Massachusetts, where almost simultaneously English General Thomas Gage plotted the removal of military stores from Concord. However, unlike Dunmore, Gage was thwarted. Thanks to the speed and persistence of Paul Revere, militiamen were alerted in time and engaged the British at nearby Lexington, where the first shot of the American Revolution was fired. News of that encounter reached Williamsburg in a remarkably short time.

During the week which had just passed, townsmen drilled and stomped out their fury on Market Square; Patrick Henry arrived with a company of armed farmers from Hanover County demanding that the governor either return or pay for every item removed from the citizens' powder magazine. Dunmore paid. But it was too late; his cooperative effort only spurred the enmity between him and the Virginians.

Even Wythe—calm, rational, meticulous clerk of the House—donned "a hunting shirt, carried a musket, and joined in military parades." There can be no doubt that his role behind the scenes was prominent, that he agreed with the machinations of the secret Richmond gathering of representatives and with the advice a reckless Jefferson had dared articulate. Parliament must stop meddling in Virginia's internal affairs. Now, George Wythe flaunted his individual disrespect for "tyranny" by marching about the capital with able-bodied freemen of assorted ages and classes. No one could doubt that he was an activist, a revolutionary.

Spring and summer of 1775 exploded with change. The April happenings in Massachusetts and Virginia set off battle preparations by both the English and the colonies. Still, that June, when the earl of Dunmore called the House into session, the external ceremonies varied little. The governor must have realized, with an inner shudder, that Speaker Randolph had had an identical role at the undercover convention in Richmond; that the militia, of which he, Dunmore, was supposed to be commander-in-chief, was recruiting at a startling rate; that his neighbor, Wythe, had joined the common rabble. Even George Wythe was the enemy.

As Professor Benjamin Quarles underscores, ". . . the crown's Representative in Virginia would have been a marked man no matter how circumspect his behavior." Lord Dunmore, no fool, measured hostility in the colony with the accuracy by which he gauged wind gusts. From his country place southeast of the capital he escaped on the H. M. S. *Fowey* later that month and sailed down the York River toward Norfolk. The inlets of Wythe's home peninsula were doubtlessly as familiar to the governor as his own fingers. Along the way Dunmore raided a few plantations, taking slaves with him. If he stopped off at Point Comfort, directly across Hampton Roads from Norfolk, he might have expected the customary welcome. Not now, because throughout

Map of Williamsburg in the 1770s.

the Revolutionary years, resistance by the Hamptonians made it a risky place for the British. His Majesty's fleet, operating out of the excellent Norfolk port, provided refuge, however; and by fall, Dunmore, in an effort to take command again of the colony's military forces, declared martial law. From his point of view there was no other alternative; the Virginia militia were traitors. Now safely aboard another warship, *William*, he put into motion a plan to enlist troops whose loyalty was insured because they wanted the freedom he offered more than life.

The plan had been hatched with the approval of his superior, Lord Dartmouth, months before. Possibly it dated from the rebellion implicit in that first secret Richmond convention. Was it then he began plotting how he could best thwart the Virginia leaders? Dunmore's dealings with the western Indians had encouraged a confidence that he could persuade them to follow him, and if he offered freedom in exchange for service in England's royal forces, black slaves, too, would be enlisted. The wily Scot could kill two birds with one stone: fill up his fighting ranks and at the same time rob the planters of their work force. What better way to cripple the Virginians' revolt? Who would work their farms, guard their families after the Negroes deserted them? And, even more significant psychologically, what if the lure of freedom triggered uprisings and wholesale murder in those regions where white folk were the minority? While Dunmore had yet to proclaim the plan publicly, rumors had the same effect as the act. Currents of panic swept the colony. Washington estimated Dunmore's potential effectiveness as ". . . the most formidable enemy America has; his strength will increase as a snowball by rolling . . ." unless the slaves and servants could be kept on the plantations.

Aware that Dunmore was within easy reach of Chesterville, Wythe shared the anxiety of other planters in the area. A few years before, the construction of a new country house for Elizabeth and him had been begun on the property. Hampton legend claims that Jefferson designed the brick two-and-a-half story building with offices below the thirty-foot-wide porch. Reconstructed floor plans and models suggest an Italianate country

villa with three lofty, evenly proportioned arches dominating the
south elevation.

But the house would not serve Dunmore's purpose nearly so
well as would Chesterville's slaves and crops and livestock. To
make matters worse, Wythe suspected that his manager, Hamilton Usher St. George, was a Tory whose sympathies were an
open invitation to Lord Dunmore.

Even more important matters commanded Wythe's attention,
however. Instead of riding south to Chesterville, he and Elizabeth departed Williamsburg that August of 1775 for Philadelphia,
the fabled city so familiar to the Keiths and Walkers, his mother's
family. The Peyton Randolphs preceded the Wythes by a day,
northward, along a route probably used by Washington on his
travels between the capital and Mt. Vernon—Williamsburg to
Gooch Ferry, Hobbs Hole, Port Royal, Fredericksburg, Colches-
ter, Alexandria, on northeast to Baltimore (called the "Damndest
Hole in the World" by delegate Robt. Morris), Wilmington,
Chester, Philadelphia. Philadelphia was the largest city in the
colonies. By the time the exhausted and dusty Wythes drew up
to their lodgings across from the city's crowded public house, the
Indian Queen, it must have seemed that all of Philadelphia's
thirty thousand inhabitants were passing in the brick-paved
streets. The contrast with the village atmosphere of Williamsburg was astonishing. Only the muggy miasma and insects reminded the Wythes of home.

Here the Continental Congress would soon be in session
chaired by Randolph, while George Wythe, less visible than his
imposing colleague, worked tirelessly behind the scenes with the
forward men from the other colonies. George III had just declared the colonies to be in a state of rebellion; so the work of the
Congress was more than urgent, it was now dangerous.

Independence was *not* uppermost in the minds of most delegates. Rather, they were meeting again because it was finally
clear that their survival hinged on interdependence. Their decisions on defense and trade must unite them against England,
overriding the interests of individual colonies. Those interests

were quite as diverse as they are in today's Congress, depending upon the resources, trade outlets, and the temper of the people's representatives. Had a Gallup poll been taken, about one-third of these gentlemen would have appeared opposed to anything resembling revolution, while another third were "very high for liberty," a phrase describing Carolina's Rutledge. This left a considerable number who were passive. These estimates were made by none other than John Adams, practiced head-counter. (There are contemporary historians who figure in retrospect that a mere 10 percent of America's population were active revolutionists. Small wonder that Virginia's rebel, Richard Henry Lee, made effective propaganda of the fact that the Congress represented 2,200,000 citizens who were expected to contribute £80,000 in revenues for the crown.)

Wythe and Adams perhaps best symbolize the compatibility of the Massachusetts and Virginia liberty men. Adams had a provincial view of Southerners and may have been surprised that the venerable lawyer from Williamsburg turned out to be one of the "new faces" he liked best. Contrary to Adams's preconceived notion that a vestryman in the Church of England was automatically a Tory, he found that he and Wythe agreed on "enlightened" religion along with the character of their future government. "Sink or swim," America must be on her own, and if that meant severing all ties with the British Empire, so be it.

These two patriots strolled the Philadelphia streets together and talked away the nights in the London Coffee House at Front and Market Streets, the favored recreation of many delegates, swapping back-room gossip and erudition, an exercise in oneupmanship both men enjoyed. In his mind, Adams probably contrasted these conversations with those he had deplored during his stop-off in New York. True, New York was a splendid, prosperous city, but its first citizens lacked breeding and modesty; they talked "loud and fast." Wythe wouldn't know about New York; Philadelphia was the farthest he had been from home. He and Elizabeth had been entertained until they came to wonder whether or not the Philadelphians ever stopped eating. The sweets were far too rich for George's palate—trifles and tarts, custards, floating island, creams and curds. Adams, accustomed to plain fare, was sampling the elaborate cuisine, including the vast variety of alcoholic beverages with the zest of discovery, and was gaining weight. The temperate Mr. Wythe probably suggested a diet and more exercise.

Adams also had ample opportunity to give Wythe firsthand observations of the very first session of the Congress. No doubt he described a tense moment between the two Virginians, Benjamin Harrison, his very bulk and finery suggestive of his vast properties, and Patrick Henry in homespun gray, disheveled, his wig unpowdered, his drawl unrefined, eyes flashing, contemptuous, demanding, "Where are now your landmarks, your boundaries of colonies? We are in a state of nature, Sir!" The many lawyers in the Congress recognized John Locke's phrase *a state of nature*, meaning that man owed allegiance to God alone, no one else, including His Majesty George III. Personal liberty was every man's natural right. John Locke, Harrington, and Montesquieu had expounded the laws of nature. ". . . distinctions between Virginians, Pennsylvanians, New Yorkers, New Englanders are no more. I am not a Virginian but an American!" Henry's oratory had cast a spell over the listeners, but the majority did not agree with him. John Adams did. He knew that Wythe also agreed.

However, Henry would not return to the Second Congress. Edmund Pendleton had made Colonel Henry of the First Regiment commander of Virginia's military forces, while he, Pendleton, the conservative head of the Committee of Safety, ran the colony without interference from the radicals Wythe and Jefferson in far-off Philadelphia that fall of 1775 and winter of '76.

Even at this late date, Pendleton hoped that Parliament would come to its senses and accept the reasoned arguments in favor of America by leaders Pitt and Burke.

Instead, anti-American passion mounted on the other side of the Atlantic. Samuel Johnson called envoy Benjamin Franklin "Master of Mischief." Resourceful, patient, sagacious Franklin found no answer to the impasse and sailed for home. The Congress welcomed their elder statesman. Years before, Franklin had authored the Albany Plan when seven colonies sent representatives to meet with the "Six Nations" of Indians in an effort to enlist help in opposing the French. A cartoon of a serpent divided into sections appeared at the time in colonial publications. The caption of the cartoon was "Join or die." How prophetic Franklin's slogan had been! Here he was in the Congress, the one among the members who knew Parliament's logic firsthand: if one colony defied the parent government, others would follow suit. The king's "state of rebellion" declaration made clear such a risk was no longer in the cards. Negotiations had ended. Not only would America be punished with a trade blockade, she must support a war against friends and brothers.

Adams put forward Washington to be commander-in-chief of a Grand Continental Army, much to the annoyance of John Hancock who fancied the role. According to letters to his wife Martha, Washington did not want the job. He considered it beyond his ability; nevertheless, he attended Congress in uniform. He must have known that he was a glamorous figure and that it would take a Southerner to enlist southern troops. This was John Adams' reasoning exactly. He also figured that Washington's wealth gave him independence.

On the second motion, Congress voted for the Virginian unanimously. General Washington must somehow coordinate the bemuddled colonial forces. Wythe was his replacement in the Congress. Time was running out. To the south, Dunmore had acquired a small raiding fleet. To the north, the English had gambled a thousand men taking Bunker Hill, burning Charlestown. The fall of Quebec would follow.

Surely the mounting colony losses would lift the Congress out of factional quagmires, "juvenilities," time-wasting pettiness. A good listener, George Wythe probably heard all of Adams' complaints, including the New Englander's exasperation with the conservative New Yorkers and Pennsylvanians, especially the Quakers, who had opposed the Continental Association boycott. Trade with the enemy did not touch their consciences. Aware of powerful Quaker trade connections abroad and their traditional underground which gathered information useful to most governments, Wythe's viewpoint may have been more tolerant though there is no way to know that. Certainly, he was pleased by Adams' enthusiasm for young delegate Thomas Jefferson. ". . . he soon seized upon my heart," was the way Adams phrased it.

Mature looking for his thirty-two years, Jefferson surpassed in scholarship and reputation many of the older delegates. They were impressed by his *Summary View of the Rights of British America*, a pamphlet widely distributed before he ever appeared in the Congress. Once there, it was soon recognized that he was no Patrick Henry or Edmund Pendleton on his feet, nor did he have the forceful manner of Richard Henry Lee. But his writing facility and style brought words to quick life, and no matter how abstract the ideas behind them, his words were as explicit as they were eloquent.

No one knew better than Wythe how quickly his prize student had developed since entering the Virginia House of Burgesses six years before. It had been at that same session, conscious of the resentment created by the Stamp Act, Townshend Acts, and other restrictions, that the then newly arrived Governor Botetourt had complimented the Virginians warmly in his first speech to them. The reply from the Assembly had called for the utmost in diplomacy. Pendleton headed the committee which would draft that reply. He had selected Thomas Jefferson for the job, but Jefferson's draft did not suit the committee who then approved another by a senior member. Thomas Jefferson's bill for emancipation of slaves did not stir a ripple, either. Between such an inauspicious debut on the political stage and the Second Continental Congress, Jefferson had acquired the responsibilities of a wife (a young widow, whose child by her first husband died within the year), two daughters of his own, had begun serious work on Monticello, and had inherited from his wife's father 11,000 acres of land and enough slaves to work it. Obviously these domestic duties had not precluded his intellectual pursuits, nor had his sudden wealth dampened his fervor for democracy. He and friend Wythe, stimulated by the heterogeneous Congress, put forward their radical theories of government in committee after committee from morning to night.

Wythe was consulted on legal and administrative details touching everything from printed money to saltpetre. (He was naturally concerned with the lack of response to Washington's desperate need for supplies.) Once a judge of the vice admiralty courts, Wythe helped decide policy when English ships were captured. He worked on Indian treaties and on the use of free Negroes in the new army. And breaking with some of the leaders, he pushed for opening American trade "altogether." He saw no *good* reason for restraining it. The Dutch, French, German, Cubans, and their neighbors were agreeable. Excluding England would enrage Parliament, but he no longer revered that august body. "Turn your eyes to Concord, Lexington, Charlestown, Bristol, New York; there you see the character of Ministry and Parliament," he insisted. The embryonic government in Philadelphia could expect only punishment, not loans from a rejected parent. British armies and men-of-war holding the Atlantic seaboard were reason enough for America to have a defensive navy added to its forces, in Wythe's opinion. But a navy was needed equally for commerce; under the circumstances, smuggling was scarcely a sin. Look at what Dunmore was doing with four ships. All of southern Virginia and Maryland was harassed by that "puking rascal" boldly raiding plantations of crops and slaves.

Whether the Congress, more absorbed in minutiae than issues, recognized the fact or not, a group of radicals was emerging. New Englanders were, of course, John and Sam Adams. Among the Southerners, George Wythe. They were men who no longer hoped for reconciliation with the empire of King George III.

X

RESOLUTION: 1775–1776

•

*Dunmore's Ethiopian Regiment fails. Virginia proposes "free and indepen-
dent States." Jefferson writes the Declaration. He and Wythe sign for
Virginia.*

City life had been far too lavish and hurried, the Wythes realized. Philadelphia's glamour paled as they drove into Williamsburg past Waller's place, past the capitol building. The Duke of
Gloucester Street was broad and uncluttered; no tall buildings
narrowed it or hid the old landmarks—the Raleigh, the courthouse on Market Square, the church corner where their coach
turned then drew up before the perfectly balanced façade of their
own home. Even the slope of the roof was friendly. It was too late
for the figs and wild blackberries. Rock fish ran this time of year
up in the York river. George Wythe's thoughts were at once free
of nit-picking politicians, new friends, and strangers. His roots
were here in Tidewater Virginia. Coming home cheered and
exhilarated him. Only now did he know how much he needed the
congressional recess. Brief as his stay must be, he was in his own
town, his own house.

But the moment of joy was quickly snuffed out by reality, the
twists of change. War brought uncertainty, tragedy. War even
turned brother against brother, friend against friend. John Randolph had taken his family to England where his loyalties were
honorable; he wanted no part of a "patriots' revolution." This
estrangement probably grieved Wythe as much as did the death
of John's brother, Peyton Randolph, considered the most distin-

guished Virginian in the early congresses. Wythe looked across the next square at Peyton's house. Betty would be staying on. He and Elizabeth must call on her tomorrow. Betty Randolph's loss reminded him that Jefferson's wife was ailing and that the young couple had recently buried their eighteen-month-old Jane.

Sorrow and anxiety threaded the golden autumn air.

That November of 1775, Royal Governor Dunmore issued a proclamation establishing his "Ethiopian Regiment." Promising slaves their freedom in exchange for a secure future in His Majesty's service, he boldly seized Norfolk and the surrounding county of Princess Anne after routing the militia guarding Kemp's Landing. The landing was on Norfolk's Elizabeth River.

Wythe was not surprised when Dunmore finally came out and openly enlisted slaves. After all, Hampton had already sustained British attack, and in that action, patriots from the home county captured the *Hawk Tender*, an enemy pilot boat. On board were ex-slave crewmen.

The rumors of slaves flocking down to Norfolk to join Dunmore may have been exaggerations. There was no way of finding out then, and the number is still unknown. Some place the total at eight hundred, but it is doubtful that half that many actually fought with Lord Dunmore who wrote his superior that some three hundred slaves were wearing the uniform of his Ethiopian Regiment. On their coats was the slogan, "Liberty to Slaves."

The mystery remains, Why did such a relatively small number follow this royal liberator? One explanation could be that less than a month after Dunmore's proclamation, he was forced to retreat in action at Great Bridge about ten miles out of Norfolk. In half an hour his casualties added up to one-tenth of his forces. The Americans were wasting no time in ridding themselves of this "monstrous traitor." They drove him back the way he had come, and Lord Dunmore was fortunate to escape the mainland and get his troops onto British ships. The citizens of Norfolk, rather than provide "quarters and provisions" for the enemy, set their town ablaze.

The Virginia Convention issued a declaration urging slaves to return to their owners within ten days with the promise that they would be pardoned. Otherwise, they could expect punishment which included imprisonment, death, and, most horrifying of all prospects, being sold to the West Indies where the cruelties were worse than death.

In Philadelphia, the Congress resumed. A letter received from Washington expressed his concern that Negroes serving in his army might desert to the enemy. Wythe, back in the Philadelphia Congress for a miserable winter session, was appointed to the committee charged with solving Washington's problem. (One of the Chesterville slaves, Neptune, had apparently escaped the Ethiopian Regiment and was in the Williamsburg gaol.)

The complexities and confusion of all wars are illustrated by Dunmore's role. Loyal to his government, he promised freedom to the slaves of white masters who had defied his royal authority. At the same time, those white masters and their faithful black troops were themselves fighting for freedom from the same government.

In Canada, in Pennsylvania, soldiers of the Continental Army died for lack of arms, food, blankets, shoes, mittens, shelter, the most basic supplies. Day after day Wythe argued in the tedious Congress to obtain these basic supplies. He argued for a navy, for free trade, convinced that trade and independence were twin goals. The colonies could not attain one without the other. The time had come when they must venture alone. For too long, America had been "one of the wings upon which the British eagle has soared to the skies," Wythe reasoned. Except for England and the West Indies, American trade should now be "universal," he said, and this meant treaties of commerce with numerous foreign powers.

"In what character shall we treat? As subjects of Great Britain? As rebels?" he demanded. "Why should we be so fond of calling ourselves dutiful subjects? . . . We must declare ourselves a free people."

By early summer, delegate Wythe knew the satisfaction of having several of his pet proposals adopted by the Congress in spite of reluctant conservatives who, in the face of all evidence to the contrary, still hoped for reconciliation with King George III, whom Wythe, on the other hand, called His Majesty, "Author of our Miseries."

Export restrictions had been lifted, trade stimulated; foreign aid for the colonies was being solicited abroad, and the war seemed better coordinated. If the British had driven the Americans out of Canada, back down the St. Lawrence, the Americans had driven the "Lobsters" out of Boston. Dunmore, his forces defeated by smallpox *and* the colonials left Chesapeake waters for good. The climate was at last favorable for an orderly state convention in Virginia's capital.

Chosen by his townsmen to be their representative, Wythe wanted to leave Philadelphia for home. But he would be delayed in the national Congress while his old rival, Pendleton, managed the Assembly in Williamsburg with the same aplomb with which he had been controlling the entire colony. If Richard Henry Lee and Wythe could only persuade the Virginia body to adopt John Adams' proposal that each colony establish its own constitution independent of England, they would have the leverage they needed with those in the Congress still holding out against "the final act."

Lee wrote Patrick Henry in Williamsburg urging that a vote be taken by the Virginia representatives. After a week of debate, Pendleton (who may have been the only member sure enough of his influence and therefore confident of success) put the resolution before the Virginia Convention. The historic resolution passed, and the news was carried to Philadelphia. There, on June 7, 1776, Richard Henry Lee, "according to the instructions of his constituents," proposed to the Congress the resolution: *That these United Colonies are, and of right out to be, free and independent States; that they are absolved from all allegiance to the British Crown; and that all political connection between them and the State of Great Britain is, and ought to be, totally dissolved.*

Lee, composed, even comfortable-looking in his summer silk outfit, knew that none of his colleagues was taken by surprise; they had heard the news from Williamsburg, too. The Union flag was flying there at that very moment.

Before the obstructionists could speak up, John Adams seconded Lee's motion on the independence Resolve. But the vote turned out to be for postponement rather than passage. After days of heated debate, the postponement was extended until July 1.

Edward Rutledge, who was enthusiastic about South Carolina becoming an independent state, thought that dissolving "all political connection" with the crown was going too far, especially at this time when total revolution might be touched off by extremism. He wrote his friend, John Jay, "I wish you had been here. The whole argument was sustained on one side by R. Livingston, Wilson, Dickenson and myself (the moderates called the Cool Considerate Men), and by the Power of all N. England, Virginia and Georgia at the other." The power of all New England, Virginia, and Georgia could very well be decisive.

Wythe and Jefferson and Lee were elated that Virginia had forced the issue. Now the other members must seek instructions from their colonies, and instinct told the three Virginia legislators that any tactic for delay was not going to work.

Naturally they agreed with the compromise suggestion that a Declaration of Independence should be prepared in the event a majority vote developed when the delegates with their instructions reconvened. The document should not be a last minute-patchwork; it must be a distillation of the major points on which there was unity.

Members assigned the task were "Mr. Jefferson, Mr. J. Adams, Mr. Franklin, Mr. Sherman, Mr. R.R. Livingston." This committee decided that Jefferson should actually compose the document. There had been any number of resolves and declarations written by him with the result that congressional leaders recognized the young man's talent for "felicity of expression" in tasteful form.

To Jefferson, it seemed more logical for patriarchs Franklin and Adams to compose the all-important exacting paper, and, more than anything else, he wanted to go back with Lee and the Wythes to Virginia. He longed to be in on the fundamental shaping of his own colony's constitution, but the congressional assignment pinned him down in the stifling City of Brotherly Love.

When Lee and Wythe left for Williamsburg, the most Thomas

Jefferson could do was send along a draft of his concept of Virginia's government, an indication that it was foremost in his mind. He adapted his preamble from that document to the preamble of the Declaration.

According to Edmund Randolph, who was filling his late father's term in the Virginia Convention, that body was in confusion "beyond parallel" in their attempts to form an independent state.

Wythe arrived too late. He could not reverse decisions already made or influence the new state constitution over which he and Jefferson had worked, clarifying their priorities. Nevertheless, he offered Jefferson's draft. It could serve as a model for revisions at least. But men like Pendleton and Henry, by now conservative compared with Jefferson and his teacher-mentor, stuck by their own version, imperfect as it might be.

Had Jefferson's constitution arrived sooner, it would have been rejected, undoubtedly. The extreme tenets he put forward such as separation from England's church, free education, manumission of slaves, and broader voting rights would disintegrate a society. The Virginia conservatives were positive of that. Severing ties with the mother country was distasteful enough.

Apparently, a political "arrangement" was still in operation. Patrick Henry was elected governor, while Wythe, the Lees, Nelson, and Jefferson were elected again to the national Congress. Those of one persuasion would control the state; their opposites, the Congress. Henry was relieved that Jefferson had stayed in Philadelphia.

In that hot, hazy metropolis, Jefferson worked on many assignments, coming back to his rooms often to write and rewrite the Declaration. He later claimed that he made no attempt at originality of principle; he simply harmonized the sentiments of the day in the briefest, most lucid way possible although "it was intended to be an expression of the American mind." Franklin and Adams made a few word changes and backed the version Jefferson submitted in the Congress, June 28, 1776.

Other members were more cautious. Some objected that Jefferson's denouncement of the king, the royal government, and His Majesty's Church were overly long. And "censures" of the English people must be struck. (That they were worth keeping as friends, Jefferson thought a "pusillanimous idea.") The Yankee slave traders and the Deep South slave owners also objected when they read his indictment of George III for warring "against human nature itself" in the delicate matter of slave trade. It was scarcely fair, they agreed, to blame the king for an institution from which Jefferson himself profited.

Hours of debate on such details insulted and bored the author . . . "these gentlemen continued their depredations," their changes were "mutilations."

Still, the final document was a finely honed symbol of unanimity, towering above narrow regional rights, its theme fluid and strong though condensed, comprehensive in less than 1500 words, vital in its philosophy of civilized freedom, focusing the vision of mankind's greatest minds.

But the miracle was that it was adopted, not merely by a majority, but by all of the American colonies: *The unanimous Declaration of the thirteen united States of America.*

Wythe, still bogged in the Virginia Convention, did not reach Philadelphia again until September. That was when he added his signature, apparently not hesitating to write it above rather than below the names of those Virginia delegates present on July 4, 1776.

To him it may have been less sacred than we contemporary Americans tend to make it. It was little more than a legal form. The substance was yet unproved. There was the phrase *consent of the governed.* Wythe liked it better than ever. *Governments are instituted among Men, deriving their just powers from the consent of the governed.* The tyranny of George III and his abuse of the law were spelled out. Thomas Jefferson left no doubt in the king's mind. *He has refused his assent to laws, the most wholesome and necessary for the public good.* Then followed a list of abuses. *He has combined with others to subject us to a jurisdiction foreign to our constitution, and unacknowledged by our laws; giving his assent to their acts of pretended legislation:* . . . *For cutting off Our trade with all parts of the world*

. . . For imposing Taxes on us without our Consent . . . For depriving us in many cases of the benefits of Trial by Jury . . .

The premise was sound, Wythe agreed. The king was guilty in every case, and the conclusion was a just one. *We, therefore . . . the Representatives of the United States of America, in General Congress, assembled, appealing to the Supreme Judge of the world for the rectitude of our intentions, do, in the Name, and by authority of the good People of these colonies, solemnly publish and declare, That these United Colonies are, and of Right ought to be Free and Independent States.*

"Independent States" was twice repeated before the final phrase, *we mutually pledge to each other our lives, our Fortunes and our sacred honor.*

Every Virginia signer was a lawyer:

> George Wythe
> Richard Henry Lee
> Th Jefferson
> Benjamin Harrison
> Thomas Nelson Jr.
> Francis Lightfoot Lee
> Carter Braxton

XI

POLITICIAN AND PROFESSOR:
1777–1781

•

*Speaker of the House Wythe. Judge Wythe in Chancery Court. Professor
Wythe at the College of William and Mary. The Revolution closes in.*

In the spring of 1777, George Wythe was returned to the Virginia General Assembly. Once more he was Williamsburg's representative. The unanimous choice of the town's eminent signer can be interpreted as a gesture of the utmost gratitude for his resolute work in the national Congress.

He had been replaced in the Congress by Mann Page in January, which means he spent only a short time in Baltimore where the delegates had fled when the British advanced too near Philadelphia. In retrospect, John Hancock, the president of that harried session, felt the move over to Maryland had been cowardly, had depressed public morale. It seems that only Quakers and critically wounded soldiers remained in Philadelphia until Washington, finally granted authority to make his own decisions, made his celebrated crossing of the Delaware and won the critical battle of Trenton.

Wythe had finally seen one of his major proposals carried out by Congress despite the general ennui of that body: the appointment of the new country's first mission to France. Benjamin Franklin, Silas Deane, and Jefferson were the delegates. Wythe was confident that these gentlemen could persuade Louis XVI to give America aid. And while treating with French diplomats, there would be ample opportunity for contacts in their embassies with representatives from other countries. But Jefferson did not sail with his fellow diplomats. He seemed almost more worried about Virginia's constitution than his wife's ill health, the reason he used for not going to France. Instead, he reentered the Williamsburg scene, and, at Wythe's invitation, lived in the Wythe home until he and Mrs. Jefferson found their own quarters in the capital.

No longer a novice in politics, Jefferson boldly put before the Virginia legislature a bill incorporating the revisions he and George Wythe felt the state constitution needed. With persuasive skill gained from his experience in Congress, he pushed the bill through, and by the time his friend Wythe came home from the Baltimore Continental Congress, the Virginia Assembly was ready to appoint a committee charged with the monumental task of revising the colonial laws.

Jefferson, Pendleton, George Mason, Thomas Ludwell Lee, and Wythe made up the committee. Although this seemingly interminable work and the resumption of his practice kept Wythe busy, there is no doubt he missed the crises and stratagems of the Continental Congress. But his election to the Assembly the spring session of 1777 soon quickened the tempo of life again.

Mason had wearied of the constitutional revisions; Thomas Lee had died; and in March, 1777, Edmund Pendleton was permanently crippled when he fell from a horse and dislocated a hip. He walked with crutches the rest of his life. Jefferson now saw an opportunity for his progressive clique to grab the power which Pendleton and Henry had long controlled. Decisively, Jefferson seized the leadership of the Virginia Assembly, and his "able and constant associate," Mr. Wythe, became speaker of the House of Delegates, the position Pendleton had used to dominate Virginia politics. This surprising turn of events intensified the rivalry between the two great jurists, and when the fall term opened, the conservatives took their revenge. Scarcely enough delegates showed up to do business even though major legislation was on the agenda, for instance, the emergency need for effective recruitment methods. One would think that a leading state in a new country fighting a revolution would be replete with volunteers. Not at all. One would think that if there were no volunteers, then a draft would, of necessity, be automatic. Not at all. Only after bitter and drawn-out debate did a draft law squeak through the legislature.

The issue of taxation was equally unpopular, but how else could Virginia raise money to sustain its government? Wythe, while a member of the Congressional Treasury Committee, had known the money problems of the country as a whole. Suppliers to the army overcharged for their goods and monopolized the profits. Inflation was making life wretched for the poor. The supply of paper money was excessive. At the same time, that money never purchased enough supplies for the Grand American Army. Now, in the Virginia House, Wythe, drawing on wide experience, helped spell out the necessity for property taxes. The taxation law passed, as did Jefferson's proposed legal system. A Chancery Court and a reorganized General Court would be set up; the former amounted to the State Supreme Court; the General Court would decide on cases of common and criminal law.

There was no end to the items on which the legislature must act. Agitation in the vast western area was flaring up between the Indiana Company and the Henderson Company, both openly ambitious to take over the rich territory. Wythe considered it Virginia's rightful possession accorded by the original charter. The British, victorious in Canada, took advantage of the conflict and moved down the frontier inciting Indians to wipe out Virginia settlements along the way.

The man who came up with a scheme for counterattack was George Rogers Clark. Interestingly enough, he, along with Daniel Boone, had surveyed and scouted for Lord Dunmore on his western campaign. Wythe, Jefferson, and Mason persuaded Governor Patrick Henry to back Clark's plan for luring each fighting man westward with a promise of three hundred acres of the land he would help Virginia keep. The property "bait" worked and Clark's campaign saved the wilderness lands from the British.

Meanwhile, General Washington, outnumbered, resorted more and more to guerrilla tactics to save his troops and supplies.

He was going begging for support in spite of a few military victories. The national Congress, by now poorly attended with the goal of independence behind them, was tired of the revolution. Small wonder that Washington charged that "speculation, peculation, and an insatiable thirst for riches seems to have got the better of every other consideration."

To the general of the Grand American Army it seemed that even his old friends Wythe and Jefferson had chosen the easier roles of staying home, focusing on the business of Virginia rather than the more important affairs of the Union. No one saw more clearly than Washington the new nation's need for its best minds.

But Wythe was content. He and Elizabeth belonged in Williamsburg. His latest appointment, along with Pendleton and Robert Carter Nicholas, was to the bench of his state's first Chancery Court. Once more, the choice was unanimous. Once more, he could bury himself in the law without the diversion of politics.

Not so in the case of Jefferson, who in 1779 was elected the governor of Virginia. By virtue of that top office, Jefferson became a member of the board of the College of William and Mary, giving him the opportunity he wanted to press for immediate reforms. Conveniently, the last of the ardent Tory presidents, John Camm, had been succeeded by a young minister. Not yet thirty, the Rev. James Madison, second cousin of the future president of the same name, shared Jefferson's vision of converting the college into a progressive, first-rate university. Certainly Madison, once Wythe's student agreed with Jefferson in the creation of a new course of study, Law and Police, and with his choice of their former professor to develop it as his wisdom dictated. They could not have conferred a higher honor. We know that George Wythe considered his appointment to the first professorship in the law school one of the most creative undertakings of his entire life.

From the beginning, he attracted "numerous" students and, according to an elated Jefferson, brought the school "universal applause." Wythe's advanced ideal for the law courses was spelled out in a letter John Adams received from him: ". . . to form such characters as may be fit to succede those which have been ornamental and useful in the national councils of America." In his mid-fifties, his most active years on the national stage behind him, Wythe foresaw the need for qualified leaders.

This may have been precisely what Madison and Jefferson had in mind when they established the new chair of law, and the methods Wythe evolved did produce the men of reason Virginia needed during a decade of disruptive transition.

John Dewey's philosophy of instrumentalism does not seem as original as educators thought at the beginning of the twentieth century when compared with the utilitarian processes of learning tested at William and Mary in Wythe's moot courts and assemblies. In 1780 his techniques were both pragmatic and experimental.

Because the war was shifting nearer to Williamsburg, the state government convened in Richmond. This left the capitol court room available for Wythe's "staged" classes, the very surroundings lending authenticity to the scene. He assigned cases to the students which they prepared and debated. Wythe and other professors presided over the "court," and the young men tested their expertise "with elegance, method and learning," before an audience of engrossed Williamsburg citizens.

In addition, there were sessions imitative of the legislature "consisting of about forty members." Professor Wythe presided as speaker of the House (as he in fact had been), sitting in a high-backed chair on a "throne," teaching parliamentary procedures in the simulated "real-life" atmosphere. Committees drew up bills and were then given "the greatest freedom" to debate and revise those bills. These laboratory classes often met on Saturday. One student wrote his father that the Saturday he "delivered an oration for the first time" was the day of his "political birth."

There is no indication that the professor's enormous prestige and scholarship intimidated the youthful tyros. Rather, the relationship built on mutual respect was also one of affection. The mature man communicated spontaneously his love of the law and his love of fellow human beings whether in the classroom or in his own study at home.

This was the exuberant Wythe many of his contemporaries

General Court room in the restored capitol building in Williamsburg. Wythe set up his law classroom at the College of William and Mary to resemble this room. *Courtesy of the Colonial Williamsburg Foundation*

failed to discover, especially those who complained about his pedantry, his self-righteousness, and his radical beliefs.

On Tuesdays, Chancellor Wythe lectured on Blackstone who wrote that "Law, in its most general and comprehensive sense, signifies a rule of action, and is applied indiscriminately to all kinds of action, whether animate or inanimate, rational or irrational. Thus we say, the laws of motion, of gravitation, of optics, or mechanics, as well as the laws of nature and of nations. And it is that rule of action which is prescribed by some superior, and which the inferior is bound to obey."

When Wythe, the young man, began his legal studies, Blackstone was not yet published (the preface to his text is dated 1765), but by the '80s American consumption of Blackstone's *Commentaries* almost matched that of Englishmen because the popularized handbook on the law so simplified ancient legal expositions.

Blackstone before breakfast would be heavy fare for student or layman, but that is how a law-school boy began his day. In fact, several recorded study plans are probably a good indication of Wythe's assignments: "Blackstone, Hume or Montesquieu" until noon. Music or entertaining reading for after-dinner relaxation, then languages, science, poetry and drama—a varied intellectual menu shaping the whole of a man's thought rather than forcing upon him the choice of a specialty.

Montesquieu's *De l'esprit des lois* compared despotism, monarchy, and republic—three forms of government—with an emphasis on the separation of powers. The great French political philosopher also deplored the effects of slavery upon a society because slavery destroyed the master along with the people he owned. Underlining such progressive theory in law and government had to be the broader views of the Enlightenment. Man could control society, consequently his own destiny, not by obeying the high clergy and nobility who claimed divinely bestowed authority, but by a rational perception of the universal order and the transcendent nature of God within that order. This pursuit was every individual's right.

Did these concepts have added dimensions for those of Wythe's students who actually fought in the Revolution? Some of them left the college for the battlefield. Others returned afterwards for study with the great pedagogue. John Marshall was one of these. Back from the front, where he had been General Washington's deputy advocate, Marshall spent a brief period at William and Mary—six weeks by some estimates—in the law school. This was said to be the only formal education he received. However, he may have already known Blackstone from thorough study and practice. He would always resemble Wythe in his reputation for brilliance and integrity. But unlike Wythe, it is said that Marshall seldom traced or cited the legal authority for a line of reasoning.

Marshall was to become President John Adams' secretary of state before assuming his famous role as the fourth chief justice of the United States Supreme Court where he dominated the Court and the Constitution in the formative years of the United States government. He favored national unity guaranteed by federal power as opposed to what we now call colloquially "states rights." His interpretation of the Constitution also elevated the authority of the Supreme Court. In his opinion, that august body's decisions were final.

It is well known that Jefferson bitterly disagreed on this point since he went out of his way to attack the judiciary and to warn that it would "undermine the foundations of our confederated fabric." Whether Jefferson was motivated by politics rather than principle is controversial. Wythe, who thought the Virginia Supreme Court's authority superseded that of the state legislature, found Marshall's decisions more tolerable. On one occasion, Wythe so disagreed with the state legislature's interpretation of their Constitution, he declared, ". . . if the whole legislature, an event to be depreciated, should attempt to overleap the bounds prescribed to them by the people, I, in administering the public justice . . . will meet the united powers at my seat in this tribunal, and, pointing to the Constitution, will say to them, 'Here is the limit of your authority; and hither shall you go, but no further.' "

John Marshall was related to Jefferson, and so was Peter Carr whom Jefferson asked Wythe to educate. The fact that Peter was more like Jefferson's son than a nephew emphasizes Jefferson's continuing admiration for his old teacher who was still assigning "Herodotus, Aeschylus, Cicero, and Horace," a load Peter found excessive. Apparently, young Carr was conversant with the Anglican vs. Deist debate because he wrote that Wythe, "said to be without religion," lived out his faith "and fulfills that great command, Do unto all men as thou wouldst they should do unto thee." Wythe taught more by example than by laying down rules of behavior.

Portrait of John Marshall, first chief justice of the United States Supreme Court, who studied under George Wythe as a young man.
Courtesy of the Virginia Historical Society

One wishes for a volume of essays by his students giving their collective appraisal of this patriot who dared remain in Williamsburg at a time when the war was closing in. His concern for a dynamic academic institution in the state overrode considerations for personal safety. The ambition Wythe expressed in the letter to Adams remained primary.

There probably is no complete list of those Wythe taught who became "useful." Besides Jefferson and Marshall, there were, to mention a few, John Breckenridge, attorney general under President Jefferson; Wilson Cary Nicholas and Littleton Waller Tazewell, both governors of Virginia; Spencer Roane, judge of the Virginia Supreme Court; and Henry Clay who clerked for Justice Wythe, who, in turn, supervised Clay's reading, a most effective form of indirect teaching. Clay was U.S. senator from Kentucky and secretary of state under President John Quincy Adams.

On the military front, beginning in 1781, the war moved into the climactic stage. "We're at the end of our tether," Washington wrote Congress in April. General Charles Cornwallis, by then commanding the royal forces in the south, decided to open a fresh offensive in Virginia following up Benedict Arnold's invasion of the Tidewater. Wythe and Jefferson had supported Arnold before he turned "traitor," and there is a streak of irony in the fact that some Virginians blamed Jefferson, their governor, for Arnold's easy conquests. The governor was particularly humiliated by Arnold's occupation of Richmond, the temporary capital. Due to miscalculation, delay, poor intelligence, and failure to rally local defense, some delegates wanted Jefferson censured for neglect, but he was never officially charged. By the time Thomas Jefferson completed his second term as governor, his rating had plummeted, and Cornwallis had failed in the Carolinas even though he left the ports of Savannah and Charleston under British control. To the horror of his commander-in-chief, Sir Henry Clinton in New York, Cornwallis, quite on his own, abandoned all objectives other than the Chesapeake area. By June, he was in Williamsburg.

Where George and Elizabeth stayed at this time is not known. The college was closed, many students having joined American troops recruited for the Yorktown confrontation. The Wythes could not have fled to the plantation at Chesterville because it was only a short ride south from Yorktown. The area was teeming with British for whom Wythe's Tory overseer at Chesterville, Hamilton Usher St. George, was an active spy. St. George loyally served Cornwallis just as he had Dunmore.

There is a widely circulated story about Wythe and a group of friends out hunting in the vicinity of an inlet of the James River where Archer's Hope Creek (now named College Creek) joins the James. Instead of spotting partridge, the hunters came upon a British landing party. Their muskets loaded for game, the distinguished Americans, too old for military service, for one moment may have imagined themselves members of Ferbinger's Yorktown battalion, listening to fife and drum urge them into battle. They aimed and they fired. Their aim was so accurate, their shot so heavy, the enemy troops ran for cover and made for their ship.

If the story was passed around among the William and Mary students, it undoubtedly gave them heart when the time came for marching out of Williamsburg down the main road toward Yorktown where they would join General Benjamin Lincoln's artillery and help win glory and freedom for rebel America.

XII

SURRENDER, GRIEF, AND THE END OF AN ERA: 1781–1788

•

"The World Turned Upside Down." Wythe resumes teaching. Virginia's representative to the Constitutional Convention. Hurries home from Philadelphia upon receiving news of Elizabeth's illness. Death and desolation. Wythe plots amendments to insure that Virginia ratifies the Federal Constitution.

When today's tourists tramp the Yorktown battlefield, mentally drawing fortification lines—the parallels and redoubts of British, French, and American forces—it seems a small place indeed considering the significance of what happened there. The surrender of Cornwallis has become a symbol of the final cessation of hostilities even though sporadic fighting continued, and at the time General Washington felt his Yorktown victory held little promise of lasting peace.

Virginia's great modern historian, Douglas Southall Freeman, wrote that "It was the American's fortune at Yorktown to make the philosophy of revolution dynamic." Such is the glorification of an event and place when viewed through the lens of hindsight. Yet at the time, Washington only briefly reported Cornwallis' surrender in the document of Definitive Capitulation which he sent to Congress. The details were concise and mentioned nothing so trite as the tune played by the British on the occasion of their final disgrace, "The World Turned Upside Down." The general's report was largely devoted to praise for "the unremitting ardor" shown by his officers and men. This was a cause for wonder, even surprise; it had been only a matter of months since mutiny among Pennsylvania and New Jersey troops had threatened the survival of his army.

The Virginia government had disintegrated into utter confusion by the time Jefferson left the governorship in June, 1781, causing Richard Lee to suggest that Washington be made a dictator who could save the state *and* the union. The larger national Congress was equally bemuddled, ineffectual, and, to Washington, infuriating. Small wonder some of his "unpaid army" quit. The country had failed them. Washington complained of this long after the battle of Yorktown. In fact, by the following May, prospects for peace were still considered remote by him and by his army, and the U.S. government was the new enemy. Were Americans unable to function as a republic? Was monarchy the only authority they understood? Some of Washington's admirers thought this the case and wanted him made king. The general was shocked, the idea abhorrent. After all, the finest years of his life had been devoted to the abolishment of monarchial tyranny.

Against this background, the French who helped him at Yorktown—Lafayette, deGrasse, Rochambeau—seemed more reliable friends than the general's own countrymen.

George Wythe, of course, in whose home Washington made his headquarters before moving into position at Yorktown, never faltered in his support. However, after the battle, Wythe's concern for the college is more specifically recorded than any concern he might have felt for Washington's men. "A few days after the reduction of York" Wythe and college president Madison called on the general with a request that the hospital set up in the William and Mary building be evacuated. Classes must resume as soon as possible.

In a letter to Jefferson, Wythe relayed this news without any reference to the Yorktown victory. He was pleased that his law school would reopen in two or three months. During that interval of waiting, he wrote, "I know not a place at which my time would pass so happily as at Monticello." He was writing in response to Jefferson's invitation. In the same letter, Wythe referred to a horse that his friend apparently owed him. Jefferson must have planned to repay with two horses in an effort to compensate for the quality of the animal Wythe had given. But the old teacher protested, "In our dealings, you, and not I . . . ought to have the advantage, for more reasons than I can enumerate."

A visit to Monticello would have been stimulating, but it was out of the question because of the state of affairs at Chesterville. Wythe's manager, St. George, had escaped to New York City as soon as he saw the French fleet was turning Yorktown into a trap for his hero, Cornwallis. His long collaboration with the British had made St. George a wanted man; there was a price on the heads of Tory spies. Mrs. St. George accused Wythe of ill treatment when he ordered her off the Back River plantation without provisions and in the cold of winter. The mystery is, Why had he waited so long? Probably his reluctance was more practical than patriotic. It was as difficult to hire a responsible farmer then as it is now.

Another factor had been St. George's aid to the patriots as well as to the enemy, judging by Chesterville claims later presented by owner Wythe. The state owed him for potatoes, pears, a cart and oxen, beef, cider, corn, and oats. The farmers in Elizabeth City County had supplied the needs of the American troops once action concentrated in the peninsula area.

But after the Yorktown victory, St. George was threatened. Fresh patriotic zeal probably terminated several "working" relationships with Tory sympathizers. As the Revolutionary engagements focused more and more in the south, Hampton had become the natural headquarters for the Virginia navy. The French, some of whom were quartered there, converted the courthouse, where Wythe had presided on the bench, into a hospital.

Reportedly, he went down to Chesterville and Hampton, once hostilities ceased, to make certain the St. Georges were no longer on his farm and to hire a replacement. He would have heard much about the valor of the home county militia at the battle of Big Bethel in which his friend Colonel Francis Mallory was killed. Big Bethel was about four miles to the west of Chesterville. He would have heard, too, about the heroic slave pilot, Caesar Tarrant, who had received his freedom, an appropriate reward in George Wythe's opinion.

Once the college was fully operating again, Wythe was happy in Williamsburg doing what he loved best, teaching. Some of his students had fought in the Revolution; most of them remained his lifelong friends. He may have been jealous of the additional distraction and time required by a second revision of the Virginia law, so absorbed was he in his classes. And he worked into his schedule a strange activity never before undertaken. The one grammar school in Williamsburg closed, and Wythe began teaching languages, mathematics, and English literature to children— without pay. Communicating knowledge from one mind to another superseded all of the other great drives which this man's intellect energized. It was as though he could never give back to others enough of what he had received as a young student from his mother and from his early patron, Benjamin Waller. One circle of generosity was completed when Wythe was asked by Waller to teach his grandson Littleton Waller Tazewell. This child may have reminded Wythe of his own precocity since it is doubtful that a slow or lazy mind would have held his interest overnight. In the case of the extraordinary Tazewell boy, the instruction covered five years. But learning for learning's sake was only part of Wythe's fulfillment. He also relished the emotional stimulus of younger minds, indicating that in their company, his own remained astonishingly buoyant and elastic. During her teens, Nancy Taliaferro, Elizabeth's niece, was a member of the Wythe household. Described as "very well bred" and a "beauty" the "prettiest girl in town," she must have attracted numerous suitors who were welcomed into the social activities of George and Elizabeth Wythe. They were also fond of nephew Richard Taliaferro who would one day inherit the house in which they spent thirty-two years.

By the summer of 1786, Jefferson had served for two years as one of the ministers of state in France. His life abroad healed the long and profound depression over the death of his wife, Martha, a depression compounded when their youngest child, Lucy, died of whooping cough. But now his correspondence with friends back home was once again lively. The Wythes' relief must have been enormous.

Jefferson's book, *Notes on Virginia*, an instant success, was one of several items George Wythe requested from his friend. Your wishes are law to me, Jefferson replied in effect, and sent the book to his old teacher. Seeing in print their controversial views opposing slavery would not shock Mr. Wythe. Who else had shared them so openly through the years?

Jefferson's letters frequently contrasted the advantages of the new American society and government with the decadence of European monarchies, the desperation of the masses. Equality and liberty were organic rights, and their roots in his homeland would produce in time a model for the Western world. Of course, Wythe agreed and scarcely needed Jefferson's admonition to crusade against ignorance, for no one gave more generously of himself to "establish and improve the law for educating the common people." No one worked more consistently on revision of Virginia's law to include free education. True, there were four generations of county justices on the Wythe side of George's family tree, but there were also four generations of gifted educators on his mother's side of the family.

Always indebted to Benjamin Waller for his own broad exposure to universal ideas, Wythe was unprepared when his old friend sent for him and announced that he was dying. His final request was that George and Elizabeth take his twelve-year-old grandson into their household. George must have felt the death of his friend Waller intensely, and the pain heightened his relationship with the grandson, Littleton Waller Tazewell, who moved into the Wythe home so that his studies might continue. It could not have been easy for the sixty-year-old Wythe to leave the eager boy even when the Federal Convention was called in Philadelphia. Nor did he want to leave Elizabeth who was not well enough to accompany him, but he knew how much James Madison was counting on Virginia to lead in the adoption of his plan for a republican form of government.

As always, Wythe was among the early arrivals. Virginia was one of the few states with enough representatives to have a quorum. The enormous job before the foremost men in the country was the basic structure of the confederation of states; for example, would the country have a "single Executive" or several? But ten days passed before a minimum of delegates straggled in to organize for business.

A group of the signers of the Declaration of Independence were back as were other prominent members of the Congress a decade before. Washington was the unanimous choice as presiding officer, and Wythe naturally headed the committee for establishing parliamentary rules. The convention was just under way when word came from Williamsburg that Elizabeth Wythe was so ill that her husband must come at once.

Instead of spending the summer with colleagues in Philadelphia, he nursed Elizabeth. Only sixteen when they were married, she had devoted herself through their thirty-two years of marriage to the comfort and contentment of George who proudly said that she was "possessed of every virtue which could render her beloved." Watching her suffer and gradually slip away was an agony beyond all of the losses George Wythe had ever known.

To the delegates in Philadelphia he wrote that nothing less than Elizabeth's condition could keep him from fulfilling his appointment, but aware as he was that she could not live, he must resign. Two months later, in August of 1787, she died, and much of George's joy in living died with her. His manner was never again the same, and while he continued to show compassion to others, it was said he moved through the world as if unconscious of all that went on around him. This may be an exaggeration since it was student Nathaniel Tucker's childhood memory. Tucker also recalled the melancholy Wythe leading him to an upstairs bedroom where the boy was lifted in "feeble arms" to watch bees working in a hive on the outside of a window pane. So, leading a child into discovery and wonder went on being the old man's spontaneous response to sadness and intolerable loss.

As one would expect of a person of Wythe's intellectual vigor, even stunned by grief, he could not remain idle. A month before Elizabeth's death, he had advertised that he would open a school in the fall. By October he was teaching again. Other pupils besides Littleton Waller Tazewell were brought to live in his home, but the experiment did not work out. The noise, activity, and discipline were too strenuous for him even with the help of the servants. Faithful "Lyddy" Broadnax, who had cared for Elizabeth through the weeks of suffering, knew the master was in no state of mind to alter his habits and the household routine even though the company of the boys cheered him. Wythe soon returned to the old schedule of regular hours when students came to the Wythe house for instruction.

Everyone knew that a convention would soon be called in Richmond because Virginia, along with the other states, must ratify the national Constitution. The voters in each county would elect two candidates as their representatives to Richmond, and *anticonstitutionalists* were determined that their view would be heard. Since Patrick Henry was their spokesman, not only would their views be heard, but the contest promised to be spirited.

In an effort to nominate an objective, fair candidate, Wythe's name was raised by the Williamsburg townsfolk. And even though he had not presented himself as a candidate, he was elected. This singular development became more conspicuous when the anticonstitutionalist candidate, General Thomas Nelson, led a procession of citizens up the street along the Williamsburg palace green and stopped before Wythe's home. The old man was giving a Greek lesson when the general knocked. He may have found it difficult to adjust his line of thought to follow what Nelson announced to him in a clipped little speech, but it was plain that the people still wanted the judge to serve them.

It was possibly the last thing Wythe would have chosen, involving himself again in public service, but he was moved by this demonstration of devotion. Outside his home, standing beside the general, he thanked the crowd. He could not refuse them.

And so it was that when Virginia's ratification convention opened in Richmond the summer of 1788, George Wythe was unanimously made chairman of the Committee of the Whole, yet another function concerned with parliamentary form. Not only was the position an honor, it indicated the aging man's superiority when it came to organizing the business at hand.

For identical reasons, Edmund Pendleton, his old-time adversary, was made president of the convention. The long-time professional rivals were now tentative allies. Virginia could be the ninth state to ratify, in which case the national Constitution would be adopted. Once more the Old Dominion was in a position to influence the future of the country.

From the beginning, the strategy of Wythe and Pendleton won out over that of the opposition leaders, Henry and Mason. Patrick Henry tried to dominate the proceedings with his most effective, dramatic weapon—speech. On some days Henry spoke six to eight hours—prophetic of congressional filibusters—and, as always, the listeners marveled. The best known of these addresses was called "We the People," a phrase ironically now familiar in the Preamble of the Constitution:

We the People of the United States, in order to form a more perfect Union, establish Justice, insure domestic Tranquility, provide for the common defence, promote the general Welfare, and secure the Blessings of Liberty to ourselves and our Posterity, do ordain and establish this Constitution for the United States of America.

The principles at stake were complex enough that volumes have been written about them. But a paragraph from historian William Clarkin's exposition of Virginia's role in ratification sums up the pivotal issue. Clarkin writes that Henry "held forth that the people by no means were creating the instrument, as the Preamble to the Constitution words it. On the contrary, the thing was done by the states. And Henry was right. But if the Preamble had been written as 'We the States,' truly a confederation would have been the result. The agreement would have been a contract between states." Clarkin concludes that "this would have meant a confederal, not a unitary, centralized government springing directly from the popular will." Henry's argument favoring a confederacy was opposed by the pro-constitutionalists.

Since there is a considerable percentage of American voters who agree even now with Henry's argument, it is no surprise that the Virginians debated vociferously through twenty-two days. It is also not surprising that the popular vehicle of compromise—amendments—decided the outcome. Who offered the amendments? George Wythe. His skillful maneuvers resulted in a close vote which was carried by the constitutionalists.

Had the antiforces won, it is conceivable that other states would have followed suit, and the Constitution as we know it would not have become our instrument of national government.

None other than James Madison, often called the father of the federal document, gave Wythe credit, along with a half-dozen other delegates, for the successful ratification. The elder statesman from Virginia, who wanted most to be left to his teaching in quiet, post-Revolution Williamsburg, had once more fought with the giants of Virginia's courts in the most refined abstractions of the law, and won.

XIII

CULMINATION: 1788–1806

•

George Wythe, sole judge of the Chancery Court. Rivalry with Pendleton and conservatives renewed. From Williamsburg to Richmond, a permanent move. To the Electoral College. Thomas Jefferson, president of the United States.

In 1788, the year Virginia ratified the Constitution of the United States, the state Assembly instituted a Supreme Court of Appeals which would function separately from the Chancery Court. The latter was Wythe's sphere of influence while his long-time rival, Edmund Pendleton, moved into the new court. This was a startling event since from that position Pendleton would have the power to review and reverse Wythe's decisions.

The new development must have been one of the most galling ironies Chancellor Wythe ever endured. Their competitive differences on the bench continuously flared even though they had effectively cooperated in getting the national Constitution adopted. In his definitive biography of Judge Pendleton, scholar David John Mays examines in detail the reasons for this long-running feud. Mays points out that one hundred and fifty cases were appealed from Chancellor Wythe's court to Pendleton's. A humiliating number for the two great jurists to contest. There are references to Wythe's "outbursts," "biting sarcasm," to his printed volume of *Remarks* on these reversed decrees as "inexcusably acrimonious and lacking in restraint." In one of the cases, Wythe attacks Pendleton's reasoning as "an euthymema, an imperfect syllogism." The display of pedantry is condescending, to say the least. On the other hand, Wythe admits his errors with disarming humility.

Law students still debate the merits and defective aspects of Wythe's *Remarks* and are influenced by the contrasting personalities and procedures of the two men. On the same grounds the contemporaries of Wythe and Pendleton were influenced.

Referring to himself, Pendleton used phrases such as "first rank," which cannot be questioned, but the self-image he draws is suspiciously flawless. Having "attained the highest office" in Caroline County as well as in the judiciary, he explains his extraordinary success in these pious words: "Not unto me! not unto me, O Lord, but unto thy name, be the praise." One cannot imagine George Wythe attributing business and political successes to the Lord's "providence," then listing his own virtues, including "an upright heart, with a calm temper, benevolent to all."

Their differences in law and government may well have echoed their interpretations of "providence" and man's condition. Pendleton would fight to the end of his life for the unchanged authority of the established church, for the church to retain its glebe lands, for Virginians to continue paying taxes for the maintenance of Anglican properties.

No one opposed any form of religious tyranny more than George Wythe although his old students Jefferson and Judge Spencer Roane were more stridently indignant. The Dissenters, most particularly persecuted Baptists, had flourished under the Bill of Rights, invoking their free exercise of religion. The Dissenters had also backed the more radical political causes of Wythe. If the Revolution and America's new Constitution did not guarantee "the rights of conscience," the struggle had been a monstrous waste.

Pendleton was a man of conscience, of course, as were his opponents. However, had his conscience been imposed upon the whole people, a basic power of British sovereignty would have survived in the United States.

As to his enemies, Pendleton reckoned there were "few indeed," and he was unable to "guess the cause" unless the enemies

Title page of George Wythe's denouncement of Edmund Pendleton's reversal of his decisions as sole chancellor of the High Court. *Courtesy of the Virginia Historical Society* were "partizan." Wythe qualified; he was partisan, that he was.

While age had not affected his enormous reasoning abilities, the diminution of authority in the Chancery Court came at a time of life when a man most needs his identity bolstered. Instead, the thing George Wythe knew best—the law—would now be tested by decisions beyond his control.

Described as still brisk and erect, his face unwrinkled by age, he was thinner and bald except for a fringe of gray hair rolled above his standing collar; preoccupied in manner, it was said he did not converse for hours at a time. Without Elizabeth, the big house on the palace green would be forever empty no matter how many friends and students dropped in. (Nancy Taliaferro had married and moved away.) But there was no longer any reason for social activities. The old days of Williamsburg's gaiety, the legislative fervor, were only memories now that the capital had been moved to Richmond.

Everything was changed in his intimate surroundings, even in the town itself. He withdrew his support of the college, peevish about some of the inferior professors, the changing administration, and teaching methods which he felt encouraged stultifying uniformity rather than the unrestrained pursuit of truth.

He would not condescend to accept a federal judgeship from the first president of the new nation, George Washington, even though the appointment was offered by his old friend and client.

Wythe's interests seemed to narrow down to the teaching of several students (Jefferson's nephew Peter Carr and William Munford were two) and reading, always reading. From the continent, Jefferson sent many books. There were coveted hours for the study of new ideas and old because these days Wythe spent less time at anything he considered superfluous and seldom wrote to friends out-of-town. Arthritis in his right thumb was the excuse; nevertheless he finally taught his left hand to perform as the right one had in order to continue the work he wanted to do. He did write Jefferson occasionally and apologized for the brevity of the letters.

As the single judge of the Chancery Court, he held four sessions in the course of a year, which meant traveling regularly between Richmond and Williamsburg. Supervising the journey with servants and luggage and youthful students and trunks of books became increasingly wearing. And so he climaxed the numerous changes of this period in his life by moving permanently to Richmond.

For a man to sever so many ties in his middle sixties had to be traumatic. Williamsburg *was* his past, encompassing the most productive and the happiest years. But there is no evidence that this man in any way lived in the past. However painful it may have been for him, he left the gracious house which he and Elizabeth had never owned. Upon ending his tenure, nephew Colonel Richard Taliaferro would be the master. (And that for only a short time as the colonel died, and by November of 1791 his executors offered the Wythe house for sale to the highest bidder.)

Wythe liberated his slaves, probably those who worked the Chesterville plantation as well as the Williamsburg servants. Had he sold them, the profit would have helped with the many expenses of moving. Some went along to Richmond with him. "Lyddy" Broadnax did.

Chesterville may have been sold at this time to Daniel Lawrence Hylton who was even less reliable than the Tory St. George because Hylton defaulted on "the payment of the principal money, interest and costs." Wythe sued and got Chesterville back. By 1795 he was advertising the Back River plantation for sale "or to be exchanged for property in New York, New Jersey or Philadelphia." By then, George Wythe seemed to have relinquished all sentiment for a holding so painstakingly enlarged and improved by four generations of his family.

The same was true for the College of William and Mary since he might have continued on the Board of Visitors had he so chosen. Instead, he ended the connection which had been the most fulfilling experience of all in a rich and varied career. He did not even take Littleton Waller Tazewell, to whom he was deeply attached, with him to Richmond but arranged for an able neighbor to continue the young man's education. William Munford, who might have smoothed the jarring transition, was ill with malaria, unable to assist his teacher on that final move from the old capital. The young admirer's company could have at least eased the desolation Wythe felt upon sending his furnishings up the James and settling in a modest, strange house atop Richmond's Shockhoe Hill. Three years before Richmond was incorporated, Colonel William Byrd had advertised, April 1739, "a town" on the north side of the James "below the Falls." The ad mentioned good spring water "near the public warehouse at Shockoes."

Fair days had drawn people to the Market, and enough of them returned and settled so that by the middle 1700s, Richmond became the Henrico County seat. William Byrd III disposed of his father's real estate by lottery in 1768 which stimulated growth, and the following year Shockoe Hill was added. (In our vernacular, it was a "development.")

Once Richmond became Virginia's capital in 1779, commerce and progress sprang up along with the tobacco warehouses. The Southern Stage took travelers to North Carolina, and the post to Norfolk was regular. The *Virginia Gazette* moved as well as the legislature. "Assemblymen, judges, doctors, clerks and gentlemen of every weight and calibre" crowded the inns. The caste distinctions of Williamsburg and its quiet stateliness were left behind. Richmond's atmosphere was casual by comparison; some called it crude.

Once the capitol building opened for business in 1788, Capitol Square became the hub of activity. Walking there, down hill and up, through muddy ravines, on rustic paths, Wythe must have thought of majestic Duke of Gloucester Street with nostalgia.

At least the view from the new home of the river below and of an expanding city was spectacular. When Munford finally joined the household, Wythe probably showed him the view with childlike delight.

In Richmond, student Munford's esteem for the chancellor increased, not only as a teacher but as a friend. Wythe still demanded excellence, complaining that lawyers were being trained "without the *viginti annorum lucubrationes* of Lord Coke," therefore were mere "skimmers of law." But in the personal relationship with Munford he was generous and incredibly sensitive. It was as though every value must be distilled, every act intrinsic.

He didn't give a fig what anyone thought of his decisions; his own sense of equity must be satisfied. Popular opinion and political pressures did not shade his reasoning. The best remembered example is probably a Chancery Court case in 1793, in which Judge Wythe settled a decade-long controversy.

Once the peace treaty had been signed with England, Virginians paid off debts to their British creditors through a state loan office. The treaty stipulated full value repayment. But Virginia's currency had been so depreciated by inflation that the creditors were saddled with monumental losses. Furthermore, some prominent Virginians took the position that money paid into the loan office had supported the war costs, and once the Revolution was behind them, their debts abroad ought to be ignored—cancelled.

To the chagrin of many of Wythe's admirers, he ruled that the debts were still owing, that full payment, according to the original evaluation was due the English. The Confederation treaty superseded Virginia law. The treaty must be honored.

The old Chancellor was never forgiven for that interpretation of justice by some leading families in the state.

Possessions and externalities no longer interested George Wythe, only people of worth involved with learning and growth such as Munford, from a prominent well-to-do Virginia family, and Henry Clay, from a broken home in Kentucky, lonely and poor, but brilliant. Consistent with the teacher's belief, these young men from opposite backgrounds were equals in opportunity. At sixteen, Clay became Wythe's secretary to whom the chancellor dictated his reports of Chancery Court proceedings. These decisions Clay prepared for the printer.

Of course, Wythe could not bypass the chance of teaching young Henry Clay who would always remember the fluency and cadences of the elderly judge as he read Greek literature aloud. Although he did not actually learn the language, Clay listened with enjoyment. He was also influenced by the chancellor's crusade against the institution of slavery, though Clay would not

Portrait of Henry Clay, Wythe's secretary and student in Richmond. *Courtesy of the Virginia State Library*

follow the example in his own public career. It was a cause less and less expedient for politicians as the South's economy became irrevocably dependent upon black labor.

Wythe introduced Clay to Richmond leaders who would further the secretary's success, and from them he learned the manners of gentlemen, just as young Jefferson had learned in the select company of the royal governor Fauquier's "quartet."

Back from France and its worldly wise court, Jefferson, by the way, was making the best of an appointment he thoroughly disliked, that of secretary of state under President Washington. His own republican ideals were more popular in France where the decade of revolution had been launched than in his homeland, judging by "the trappings of aristocracy" the Federalists now exhibited.

In Richmond, one of the Federalist leaders was Wythe's former student, John Marshall. Already famous as a military officer, his popularity was immense in social, legal, and political circles.

Marshall's acceptance was at least partly due to his marriage to Polly Ambler. Her father, Jacqueline Ambler, was the state treasurer. Marshall found a small cottage for his bride and busied himself in his new law practice. A member of the Assembly, he gambled at backgammon and whist with his colleagues, who found his extroverted charm irresistible, as did Polly, especially when he brought home a hatful of cherries instead of a client's fee. But by the time his old master, Wythe, moved to the capital, the Marshalls had become prominent, moved into a large, new home where legislators in town for sessions of the Assembly were entertained and their "support" solicited.

Nevertheless, at the most important public meetings in the capital when opinion must be rallied behind President Washington on certain policies such as the one of neutrality, George Wythe presided. But during the presidency of John Adams, Wythe just as energetically opposed the infamous Sedition Act, a travesty of the freedoms the two old friends had won for their country in the early days of framing a Constitution. And when the Democratic-Republicans in Virginia picked their men for the Electoral College, Wythe was among them—a sure sign of his still vital prestige and his liberal-minded persuasions. The famous election of 1800 is a study in political chicanery, so subtle that Wythe not only disapproved, he may not have fully understood his party's tactics. The election reflected the low morale and fear prevailing in the country. In Virginia an epidemic of yellow fever and the discovery of a plot by the Negro Gabriel to massacre whites precluded politics. An equal vote in the Electoral College threw the outcome into the House of Representatives, and the balloting went on for day after ludicrous day until February 17. On the thirty-sixth ballot, Jefferson was elected with a majority of six states. The Federalist machinations caved in, and the new president entered office hoping to convert his enemies to republicanism.

Until his death, George Wythe regarded Jefferson as his best friend. Aware of such enduring affection, we can surmise the deep meaning the event held for the chancellor who must have listened to eyewitness accounts and read everything he could find about Jefferson's inauguration, including the address in which he mentioned *their* causes, "freedom of religion, freedom of press, freedom of person."

One question the third president of the United States posed is a question we ask today: "Sometimes it is said that man cannot be trusted with the government of himself. Can he, then, be trusted with the government of others?" From the ideals of liberty for which each citizen took responsibility, Jefferson was ready to gamble on an affirmative answer. The American people must attain sound government which would order their corporate affairs while guaranteeing the individual the freedom to develop any potential he might have.

Anticipating his election, Jefferson had been plying both Wythe and Pendleton with questions about parliamentary procedures in the Senate. "I am entirely rusty," he said. Wythe replied that he was too. "I have thought so little of those rules that my memory doth not enable me to supply such of them as may deserve your attention," he wrote. Nevertheless, Jefferson sent along his questions and Wythe replied, sometimes with a mere no or yea. Besides yea, there is a sprinkling of "doth" and "seemeth" and the pointed omission of capitals in reference to the "british house of commons" which reminds the reader of what Quakers call "plain language."

Aside from the legal duties in Chancery, Wythe deliberately reduced life to the simplest choices. French fashion in speech and clothes which swept Virginia probably escaped his attention. He saw fewer friends, but those who had his company expected him to wear his dated colonial silver buckles and quality broadcloth "cut in front Quaker style" with a buttoned-up long vest. In Williamsburg, hands clasped behind him, deep in thought, his brisk walk had long been familiar to the townsfolk. Now, he strolled the Richmond hills using a gold-headed cane, his step slow, his shoulders stooped. He wore glasses for reading, but there is no indication that he bothered to try George Washington's miserable experience of being fitted with false teeth, although he needed them.

He attended church services held in the legislative chamber of the capitol where two ministers alternately conducted the worship. Both became close friends of Wythe. One, a Scotsman, Mr. Buchanan, served the Episcopalians; the other, a Mr. Blair, preached to the Presbyterians. Then there was a rabbi in the Richmond Jewish community who stimulated a new undertaking. Rabbi Isaac B. Seixas of the historical Congregation Beth Shalom, a scholar and historian, taught the elderly Wythe Hebrew. From childhood George Wythe had known the New Testament in the original Greek; he must have sought fresh light from the Scriptures to have tackled the difficult Hebrew texts.

These learned gentlemen gathered at Wythe's frame house on the hill and read aloud ancient poetry in the original languages as naturally as club women sit down to an afternoon of bridge. If the day was fair, the breeze gentle, they probably first surveyed the host's garden extending along one side of the modest one and one-half story hip-roofed residence, painted a cheery yellow. Upon moving there he had planted a tree, the pyramidal *Liriodendron tulipifera* (as Wythe would have referred to it), a yellow poplar with tulip-shaped leaves. In bloom, it must have been highly visible on Richmond's Shockhoe Hill, a blaze of orange.

Oil painting of Richmond (artist unknown) from Weddell's *Virginia Historical Portràiture.* View of Richmond and the James River looking east from Libby Hill. *Courtesy of the Virginia Historical Society*

There were neighbors—Major William Duval and Dr. McClurg, the latter a teaching colleague in the William and Mary days. They and the venerable judge exchanged books and compared their experiments with mulches and new strains of seeds. Jefferson had once sent some highland rice from the East Indies, which he raised in pots. Wythe would have tested the rice, duplicating the same conditions.

By 1804, when the ambitious Jefferson ran for president again, Wythe once more sat in the Electoral College and once more celebrated the triumph of his great friend whose first term had accomplished a moderate blend of what has been labeled "reconciliation with reform." Jefferson emerged from the second campaign a popular idol of the common people, "a newfangled deity" to opposing Federalists, and the unchallenged head of the Republican party.

The vote was a runaway majority this time, inspiring the president to quote from the Parable of the Prodigal Son in reaching for an analogy to describe his joy over the united front the Republicans engineered. Those who had rejected him four years earlier joined to make his dream of "perfect consolidation" come true. Democracy rode in with the certainty of spring and was celebrated throughout the land with a lustiness absent from the American scene since independence had been declared.

In Richmond, the victory had been anticipated with elaborate day-long feasts. Cannons boomed along the capitol lawn, oratory gushed and bands blasted.

Wythe, of course, attended a gathering of the capital's inner circle of Republican first citizens. The toasts at that dinner in the Washington Tavern were endless, and the sole chancellor of Virginia's Chancery Court, modest though he was, could not conceal his pleasure when Governor John Page toasted him as well as President Jefferson, "George Wythe, distinguished alike for his wisdom and integrity. . . ."

There were nine cheers lifted for the president.

There were nine cheers lifted for the chancellor.

This occurred at a time when his eccentricities made him seem "little remote from insanity" to one observer. Despite the fact that some thought he was becoming feeble and dotty, his reputation for justice and scholarship soared, and the veneration Virginia bestowed upon him matched the glory shone upon his fellow champion of human rights, the president of the United States.

XIV

LEGACY OF FORGIVENESS:
JUNE 8, 1806

•

"Memorandum" dictated fifty years later. The cast of Wythe's Greek tragedy. George Wythe Sweney's irrational boldness. Arsenic and victim Michael Brown. The last days of a just and compassionate man.

Before the move from Williamsburg to Richmond, William Munford mentioned in one of his letters praising Judge Wythe that "he had begun to teach Jimmy, his servant, to write." Munford knew that the instruction of the Negro, Jimmy, along with the white students was a departure from current mores. But it was probably a long-standing practice in George Wythe's teaching career.

In the chancellor's Richmond household, there lived a freed boy named Michael Brown. According to George Wythe Munford, (William's son), Michael learned Latin and Greek and "the rudiments of science" under Wythe, but in Michael's case there was a difference. There was gossip that mulatto Michael was George Wythe's son by his housekeeper Lydia Broadnax, and as recently as 1974, Fawn M. Brodie's best-seller biography of Jefferson flatly referred to "George Wythe, . . . who would later be involved in miscegenation on his own part."

Ms. Brodie provides no footnote for the statement. However, it repeats one dictated by a Dr. John Dove in 1856. The so-called Dove Memorandum states that Wythe "had a yellow woman by the name of Lydia who lived with him as wife or mistress as was quite common in the city . . . By this woman he had a son named

Mike . . ." and, tutored by the almost eighty-year-old Wythe, became "an accomplished scholar."

Certainly no rational person can ignore the all-too-visible evidence of the interbreeding of races, whether in the antebellum South or in the rest of these United States today. To generalize the fact is to fall into the Freudian trap of confusing the objective world with the Eros and fantasies of the unconscious. There were and are men for whom monogamy is quite as normal as is promiscuity for others. I am convinced that at the core of Wythe's personality was an authentic preference for order and moderation, not for the sake of discipline, but rather as an expression of his innate control over all appetite, including sex, quite the same as meat. This proves nothing but is consistent with his broader morality which was as puritanical as Madison's. More significant is the absence of self-righteousness in both characters, leaving them free in their associations with others who were permissive by habit.

Since gentlemen of Wythe's tradition and class took pride in an heir who extended the family name, there seems firmer evidence of the judge's sterility, having married twice, both brides teen-aged. All sheer psychoanalytical speculation! (Dr. Dove's, Ms. Brodie's, and mine.) George Wythe's character simply does not lend itself to generalizations. Nevertheless, that Lydia Broadnax was devoted to him was fact. Firsthand observers commented that the grief of George Wythe for Elizabeth showed in his very countenance; "silent and grave," he "commanded the sympathy (even) of those who knew nothing of the cause." After Elizabeth's death his energies were focused on intellectual pursuits as never before, reportedly to the point of abstraction. Dr. William Clarkin suggests that the detached rationalism of voguish Deist beliefs was small comfort and that George Wythe returned, during those years without Elizabeth, to the religious orthodoxy of his parents.

And grandparents? Did not Grandfather Walker's Quakerism agree with the Episcopal tenet that God is immanent, personal, as well as transcendent, and that he was fully revealed in Jesus who was "the Light within"?

With property and possessions, including slaves, Wythe in his mid-sixties had simplified his entire manner of existence. It may well have been the same with his innermost spiritual refining or renewal. This seems to describe the essence of Wythe's old age on all levels of thought and relationships.

In Williamsburg, the Wythe house had been a favorite center of activity for the young. In Richmond, though the place on Shockhoe Hill was smaller and the judge's salary reduced, young people were just as attracted. For a time, a niece joined him. And there were students and beginning lawyers, and there was Michael Brown, "a child." A will drawn by George Wythe at age seventy-seven indicates how much the child must have meant to the old man. Unlike Jefferson, who shared the liberals' abhorrence of slavery but considered the black "in reason much inferior, as I think one could scarcely be found capable of tracing and comprehending the investigations of Euclid," Wythe proved through experiment that color had no bearing on the capacity of a mind to learn. If Michael, as a child, learned Greek, as reported, he may have studied Euclid.

According to Wythe's 1803 will, the three freed Negroes, who were his most intimate companions since they cared for him and his home, would receive "support" while the bulk of the estate would go to the grandson of Wythe's sister. This was namesake George Wythe Sweney who came from the low country to Richmond and joined his uncle's household.

By the time he was seventeen it was known that young Sweney was stealing and had "sold three trunks" of his uncle's most valuable law books. This undoubtedly had a bearing on a codicil which Wythe added to his will in 1806 in which he made clear that he wanted Jefferson to rear Michael Brown and use the income from Wythe's Bank of Virginia stocks to maintain and educate the intelligent mulatto boy. And while Sweney remained a beneficiary, Wythe apparently wanted to be sure that his books and "small philosophical apparatus" went to "Thomas Jefferson, president of the United States of America; a legacie, considered by my good will to him, the most valuable to him of anything which I have power to bestow."

From this codicil, it is not farfetched to conclude that the two people in the world most dear to Wythe at its writing were Jefferson and Michael who, in the event of the old man's death, he wanted to be together as teacher and student, father and son.

This document also includes a prayer substantiating Clarkin's theory of the more personal religious search. It may not have been an original prayer, but in it George Wythe asked that "penitence sincere to me restore lost innocence," that his sins be forgiven, and that when he died he might partake of eternal life.

An eighty-year-old man in the year 1806 expected death; he prepared for it realistically. But it seems that Wythe almost had a premonition that his own was near because only three weeks passed before he added yet another codicil in which he divided his bank stock equally between Michael Brown and George Wythe Sweney. In the event that Michael died first, young Sweney would receive the entire amount.

Obviously, the chancellor was still preoccupied with his most intimate possessions, not for their material worth but for their sentiment, because he added his silver cups and gold-headed cane to the objects intended for Jefferson. And his friend and neighbor who was attending to the drawing up of these legal documents, Major William Duval, would receive "my silver ladle and table-spoons."

Benjamin, the other Negro servant mentioned in the first will, had died. And, curiously, this second codicil left Lydia "my fuel."

It was wintertime—the Richmond winter of high winds and trees dripping wet from fog, and clay trails too slippery on the hills for coaches to pass. The leaden gray of winter lifted; trees turned green, and sunshine dried the trails to dust.

Then in late May, that fragrant, flowering month, the orderly routine of the Wythe household was jarred by sudden change. Everyone in Wythe's home, except Sweney, became ill. Word of Chancellor Wythe's illness spread through the town, but it may have been assumed by the public that humiliation was enough to confine the chancellor. His grandnephew, Sweney, had been taken away by police and jailed. On May 27, he had been brought into Richmond's Court of Hustings and charged with forgery.

One check was for the sizable sum of $500. All of the checks bore the forged signature of George Wythe.

The old man refused to put up bail for Sweney, set at $1,000., probably because far more than forgery was involved. So recklessly had young Sweney behaved, his uncle suspected that the youth was deranged, and while it was too late for Wythe to protect himself, the rest of society should be protected. By now he guessed that Sweney was responsible for his own worsening illness. Two days earlier, Wythe had begun his day as usual with a cold shower at sunrise, followed by the reading of some decisions he was preparing for Chancery Court; then he rang for "Lyddy" who brought breakfast of poached eggs, toast, and coffee. At nine o'clock he developed symptoms suggesting a gastrointestinal disorder. Although not recorded, it is likely there were other clues such as a burning sensation producing both thirst and excessive saliva.

Within hours, Michael and Lydia were suffering attacks identical to Wythe's of vomiting, diarrhea, and abdominal pains. Lydia survived, but Michael did not. The date must have been June 1 because on that day the weakened old chancellor, unable to leave his bed, sent for Edmund Randolph, who wrote yet another codicil to the Wythe will. In it there is a pathetic reference to Michael Brown, "who, I am told, died this morning."

The purpose of this codicil was to disinherit George Wythe Sweney. The grandnephew would receive nothing. Instead, his brothers and sisters, "the grandchildren of my said sister," would share equally in the estate. There were no further changes. The will was signed by four witnesses, placed in an envelope addressed by Wythe himself to neighbor Duval, whose letters to President Jefferson provided the basic facts that "the whole family" had been poisoned, that Michael, "the mulatto boy," was dead, and that "yellow arsenic" had been found in young Sweney's room.

Rumors of homicide raced about the capital, and a kind of awed waiting set in. How long must the poisoned chancellor suffer?

In the court records, evidence was piling up dramatically. The day before his arrest, Sweney had shown Tarlton Webb, one of the witnesses giving testimony, a paper bag of rat poison (arsenious acid was and is used to destroy vermin, rats, plagues of insects). Sweney, in a wild, desperate state, threatened to commit suicide. Under the circumstances, that was not too surprising. However, it was surprising when he asked Webb if he wanted to do the same.

On the stand, the jailer recalled that his servant had found a packet of arsenic in the garden where it had been thrown from inside the jail wall.

Another witness told of being present when Wythe dictated the final codicil of the will. At that time, the old man requested that the nephew's room be searched. Arsenic was also found there, confirming Wythe's suspicions. Now George Wythe was certain that, like Michael Brown, he, too, would die of the poison.

Of course, the one person who knew more than anyone else about what had gone on in the house on Shockhoe Hill was "Lyddy," and even though she was a freed slave, the testimony of Negroes pertaining to whites was not admitted to the record.

But she did tell what she knew to the doctor, who must have passed the information along to the two ministers Buchanan and Blair, who called regularly on the dying Wythe. What they learned was told in the sensational book, *The Two Parsons*, written years afterward by William Munford's son, George Wythe Munford, who was the same source for the information that Michael was bright and truly learning from their old teacher. Like nephew Sweney, the author Munford had been given George Wythe's name.

How faithful Munford was to the facts and how much he added out of reverence for his father's great friend and tutor, no one knows. But *The Two Parsons* is lively reading, and the account accredited to Lydia Broadnax of the poisoning, (she must have by chance received a superficial amount) simply clarifies the point that Sweney learned of the change in his uncle's will, the one leaving all of the estate to him in the event Michael Brown preceded Wythe in death. Lydia had found the nephew reading the will after having unlocked the master's "private desk." She had also seen the youth throw a small paper bag in the fire while having his coffee.

Not only does Lydia's story seem reliable; so does that of the two ministers who returned to their friend's bedside throughout his illness, to pray with him and to give him comfort. The spectacle of his agony must have been unforgettable to all who saw him, for arsenical cholera produces continuous retching of blood and bile, simultaneous diarrhea, violent thirst, spasms of the colon, progressing to a freezing sensation in the legs, and an erratic pulse, the heartbeat racing then weakening until the blood-pumping organ collapses.

On June 8, 1806, George Wythe slipped into unconsciousness, and with his two good friends, Buchanan and Blair at the bedside, passed from this rich and satisfying life to the next which the three men had discussed together in terms of the biblical promise of Christ: "I go to prepare a place for you . . . I will receive you unto myself that where I am ye may be also." One of the ministers had referred to Our Lord as "a better Friend than either of us" and asserted that the next dimension of the ongoing life would be "better than this." Buchanan and Blair were what we would now call ecumenical in their relationship and evangelical in their doctrine. Had Wythe not agreed with their beliefs by then, they would have been the last people he would have wanted near him in his final days. Without a doubt, they were welcome; their sorrow must have equalled that of Munford and Duval and President Jefferson—President Jefferson who had looked forward to the post-White House years when he and friend Wythe could indulge their leisure at Monticello.

And in a way even Jefferson could not understand, "Lyddy's" grief encompassed the affection she had known through many years for Elizabeth and George Wythe who were, in all reality, her world. Outside of that world—now that "old master" was gone—even her freedom would be meaningless.

From hill to hill, the tolling of the church bells echoed. Gradually all of Richmond knew that the respected judge and Virginia signer of the Declaration of Independence was dead, the suspense, ended.

An autopsy was performed, according to Wythe's own request, and the executive council arranged for the body to lie in state the very next day in the hall of the House of Delegates. The Virginia capitol building was packed with the citizens of Richmond and all of its dignitaries as William Munford, who considered Wythe the most remarkable man he had ever known, "the best friend I ever had . . . as kind to me as a father," gave the funeral oration in eloquent cadence: "In calling to your recollection his virtues, my own inclination would induce me to begin with those of his private life, in which I confess my own heart is more particularly interested . . ." Rather than share his subjective reverence for his friend, Munford turned instead to Wythe's public virtues: ". . . to the uncommon patriotism, which was conspicuous during the whole course of his long and useful life. The first remarkable example . . . was his conduct at the commencement of the American Revolution. In those perilous days when life, liberty and property were placed at hazard; when all that is held most dear by the mind of man depended on the doubtful issue of war; when death and confiscation would have been the fate, if they had proved unsuccessful . . .; our venerable patriot, Mr. Wythe, was firm and undaunted, and zealously attached to the cause of his country. At that important time when the greatest men America ever produced were chosen . . . to whom did his fellow citizens look . . . ? To George Wythe . . . He was one of that famous Congress, who assembled the 18th of May, 1775, and did not separate until they declared the Independence of America . . . who signed that ever memorable declaration by which they pledged 'their *lives*, their *fortunes*, and their sacred *honour*' to maintain and defend the violated rights of their country."

Munford spoke, according to the Richmond *Enquirer*, extempore of his "second father" with a fluency envied by most of the listeners: "Kings may require mausoleums to consecrate their memory; saints may claim the privileges of canonization; but the venerable George Wythe needs no other monument than the services rendered to his country. . . ."

The vast crowd attending the state funeral included the governor and the entire council, Wythe's associates in the highest courts, the mayor of Richmond, and his administrators. The people, whose rights he had so steadfastly spelled out in the revolutionary law of an independent country, the people in whose hands he believed the government could be trusted, made up the great procession solemnly following the narrow coffin down the red clay path from the capitol over to the next hill. And there, in the west yard of the Church of St. John, George Wythe was buried.

In today's metropolitan sprawl of Richmond, the capitol building no longer dominates the scene as it did in Wythe's time, but nearby still stand the monuments to his friends Washington, Marshall, Clay, Jefferson. The classic Ionic columns of the capitol building remind us that here is another of Jefferson's Greek designs ornamenting the top of a hill in Tidewater Virginia.

An engraving by Harry Fenn, c. 1872 of the St. John's Episcopal Church cemetary where George Wythe was buried without a stone. *Courtesy of the Virginia State Library*

Not long ago I drove from the capitol building to St. John's Church. The traffic was horrific; the one-way streets, befuddling. To make driving worse, my mind was on the events of almost two hundred years ago—George Wythe at work in the Chancery Court, his behind-the-scenes maneuvering at Virginia's constitutional conventions held in the Hall of Delegates. From those conventions evolved the independence and character which mingled with and influenced the government of the United States of America.

I found the churchyard of St. John's littered, uninviting. Contemporary sounds spoiled even the intimacy of death. And yet, standing before the stone bearing the name of George Wythe, I sensed the reality of him as I had—at Chesterville, at Williamsburg. The stone does not necessarily mark the actual grave. No one seems sure where it was. The peculiar turn of events after the impressive funeral have left many questions unanswered. They will always haunt me. Why did the doctors who performed the autopsy, perhaps Wythe's last request of them, fail to agree on the evidence of poisoning when they must have recognized it for what it was? They were his friends—McCaw, Foushee, McClurg. Why didn't the defense lawyers, Edmund Randolph and William Wirt, plead insanity for Sweney? They, too, were the chancellor's friends. Why did the jury, after hearing testimony that arsenic was found on the prisoner, on food, and in containers at the little yellow house on Shockhoe Hill, free the accused, declaring him "Not Guilty" of the deaths of Michael Brown and Chancellor George Wythe? And why, if Sweney were innocent of homicide in the jury's opinion, was he not held on the forgery charges? One of the checks had been signed even after his uncle had fallen into his final illness.

Young Sweney, charming though he may have been, was understandably jealous of Michael Brown, and of his uncle's attachment to the boy. His compulsive gambling had gone beyond all reason; he was desperate. The inheritance was a way out. But had he known of the will when he moved to Richmond? If so, it was only a piece of parchment so long as his uncle remained alive. Had he discovered it later and plotted Michael Brown's murder, certain that he could obtain money to support his dissipation once the mulatto was out of the way? Did he know so little about arsenic that Lydia's illness and his uncle's death were accidental? Had he intended to kill only Michael? From the mystery these questions create emerge the diagnostic signs of psychopathy: reckless chances which defied common-sense caution (the forgeries would inevitably be discovered); emotional instability (the threat of suicide in prison is not surprising, but Sweney's suggestion that his jailer kill himself as well is indeed irrational); disregard for social reactions (he knew his erratic behavior, stealing, gambling, would bring disgrace on his uncle); certainly he lied without compunction, exhibited no self-control under stress. All of these traits add up to "undue conceit," typical of mental illness.

If his family suspected this, and if Wythe's friends—the doctors and lawyers—suspected it, there is reason for suppressing evidence. There is reason for the not guilty verdict. Within the context of the times, insanity was concealed at any price and may have taken on an even more dreadful aspect than murder.

One other factor may shed light on the outcome of the case if *The Two Parsons* is a reliable source. It quotes the victim as telling his attorneys Randolph and Munford that he did not want his nephew prosecuted or punished, nor did he want "a stigma cast" upon the name of his sister. "I shall die leaving him my forgiveness," Wythe said.

Forgiveness transcends justice. Only a man whose anguish brought him grace could envision a glory beyond the law, a truth larger than any "mortal discourse." To forget such a man is a betrayal of our common legacy. Having met one of the colonies' greatest radical scholars, teachers, lawmakers—almost forgotten, one of the nation's Forward Men, a signer of the "unanimous Declaration of all the thirteen States of America"—we can better protect and nourish the concept of universal human rights which enlivened him. We can better work for a legal and spiritual excellence in our own society.

Liberty is more than a right. Liberty is a contagion, an influ-ence, a vitality springing from the mind and heart which makes real the exquisite balance between freedom and order.

The life—and grace-filled death—of George Wythe is evidence of this indestructible truth.

ACKNOWLEDGMENTS

On the evening of December 18, 1921, Oscar L. Shewmake, Esquire, addressed the Wythe Law Club of the College of William and Mary in Williamsburg, Virginia, in the informal surroundings of the Shewmake home; "a group of young men, students in the Marshall-Wythe School," requested that their professor, Dr. Shewmake, tell them something of "the great teacher, lawyer, jurist and statesman whose name their organization was to bear. . . ." That address has been the "biographical sketch" to which all of us turn when writing of George Wythe.

I, for one, took seriously Shewmake's list of qualifications any biographer of Wythe should possess: "The successful writer . . . will be a Virginian whose ancestors had some part . . . in the stirring events of the times in which he lived . . . who has labored in the several fields in which Wythe wrought so well . . . a real teacher . . . a lawyer . . . experienced in legislative work . . . a man of scholarly attainments with an understanding heart, in short, a gentleman . . . ."

I would hope that such a gentleman will fulfill these requirements and produce a definitive biography of George Wythe.

I am not a gentleman, nor do I meet the other lofty requirements; however, many of those who provided me with information do. To them, to others, who, like myself, simply value history, and to those who make it, I express deep thanks.

Historian William Clarkin, professor of history, State University of New York at Albany, and Marion L. Starkey, retired, author and teacher of Saugus, Massachusetts, really set my course by giving me carte blanche permission to use their invaluable publications. Dr. Clarkin's thesis, *Serene Patriot: A Life of George Wythe*, is the most comprehensive book on Wythe I have found. Not only did the author make available this publication, he offered to share *all* of his research material far exceeding that bound in the above title. Marion Starkey's history of Hampton and Elizabeth City County was also published as a thesis and provides many clues to Wythe's background because of Ms. Starkey's scrupulous research of court records in Elizabeth City County, Virginia.

My beloved friend, J. Logan Hudson, made it possible for me to visit the site of Chesterville and introduced me to Dr. Franklin H. Farmer. Frank remains my sharpest critic and unflagging source of enthusiasm. President of the Langley Research Center Historical and Archeological Society, he made a point of my knowing the other officers: Kitty O'Brien Joyner, Charles W. Watson, Jr., Mr. and Mrs. Jeff Cleveland II, John L. Patterson, Kenneth L. Quinn, William D. Mace, Hugh S. Watson, Jr., and the chairman, Elizabeth Sinclair Johnson. Betty, descended from the "old stock" of Wythe's home county, has supplied details about genealogy, Tidewater flora and fauna, customs, and legends unknown to "outsiders."

Kitty Joyner has typed and copied documents, cleared permissions, spent a small fortune on phone calls, tramped the environs of Chesterville with me, shared her dearest treasures (home, husband, son, cats), her remarkable acumen, and bounteous friendship. The friendship has turned many of my low moments of struggle into "highs." There is no way to say thank you for friendship except with the response of an open heart.

The vintage friendships of Mrs. L. P. Richards and Mr. and Mrs. Blake Cameron, Jr., must be mentioned here. Their generosity, dating back to the late '30s in Hampton, Virginia, has contributed much to this writing venture.

For making suggestions and answering specific questions, I thank W. Edwin Hemphill, editor, the Papers of John C. Calhoun, Archives Department, University of South Carolina, Parke Rouse, Jr., director of the Virginia Independence Bicentennial Commission, and Elbert M. ("Tiny") Hutton, administrative assistant to Virginia Congressman, Thomas Downing; Harold S. Sniffen, historiographer of the Diocese of Southern Virginia; Delegate and Mrs. Lewis A. McMurran, Jr., of Newport News; Mrs. George Pilcher, Jr., and attorney Edward P. Budnick of Norfolk.

In Virginia's capital, Richmond, I was given memorable hospitality along with professional assistance, for which I am grateful to John Melville Jennings, director, Virginia Historical Society, and his colleagues, Mrs. K. W. Southall, curator, Special Collections, Susan Agee, assistant in manuscripts, and the late inimitable Clarence Trainum; to Louis H. Manarin, state archivist, Virginia State Library, and his colleagues, John W. Dudley, head, Archives Branch, Jean Thill, assistant, Picture Collection.

The Colonial Williamsburg Foundation made available anything requested from the vast resources of that unique repository of American historical records. I want to thank especially, N. M. Merz, research archivist, Linda Rowe, Graphic Arts Collection, Jean R. Sheldon, Audio Visual Library.

I also thank William C. Pollard, librarian, Swem Library, the College of William and Mary, and Margaret Cook, curator of manuscripts there, whose antenna relaxes not, even when the lights go out.

Other specialists who came to my aid were: J. Allen Spivey, librarian, Brunswick Junior College, and his associate, Virginia Boyd; David E. Estes, assistant university librarian, Special Collections, Emory University; Walter W. Ristow, chief, Geography and Map Division, and John C. Broderick, acting chief, Manuscripts Division, the Library of Congress: Michael F. Plunkett, public services archivist, University of Virginia Library; Marjorie D. Kirtley, librarian, Virginia State Law Library; J. Isaac Copeland, director, Southern Historical Collection, the University of North Carolina Library; Lilla Hawes, director, Georgia Historical Society; Elinor S. Hearn, research assistant, the Church Historical Society, Austin, Texas; Jean F. Preston and Harriet McLoone, Americana Manuscripts, the Huntington Library of San Marino, California.

Elizabeth Rountree, director, Brunswick Regional Library,

and her colleagues, Harriett Hammond, Marsha Hodges; Fraser Ledbetter and Lillian Knight, far more than librarians to all of us who love the St. Simons Island Public Library.

Attorney L. Julian Bennet, whose loans from his splendid law library will now be returned. With apologies, I thank you, Mr. Bennet.

This manuscript has been revised more times than I care to remember and taken on numerous forms. For respecting the idea, I thank Tad and Bill, Marie and Cathy of Harper & Row. For keeping the idea alive in my own mind with their intangible, devoted support, Anna and Theo, Ann and Lady Jane, Nancy and Frances, Lorrie and Bev, Isobel and Lorah, George and Johnnie, I thank.

Elsie Goodwillie, who can actually read my handwriting, corrects my phonetic spelling, and expertly types draft after draft with everlasting patience, deserves my particular appreciation and love, as does Eugenia Price, who makes it possible for me to live and work in a creative atmosphere of reality and imagination. From her hoard of wisdom and experience, she gives with total abandon, daring. Incredible!

While *George Wythe of Williamsburg* is dedicated to Kathryn Pace Cameron, my journalism teacher at Hampton High School, who survived to become a dear and encouraging friend, the book "belongs" to my parents, Rev. and Mrs. Leroy Blackburn. Their years of ministry in The Old Dominion bound their hearts to a place and its people whom they love second only to me, and I am blessed.

SELECTED BIBLIOGRAPHY

Adams, E. D. *The Power of Ideals in American History.* New Haven: Yale University Press, 1913.

Adams, John. *The Works of.* 10 vols. Boston: Little Brown, 1859.

Andrist, Ralph K. *George Washington: A Bibliography in His Own Words.* New York: Newsweek, 1972.

Becker, Carl. *The Eve of Revolution.* New Haven: Yale University Press, 1920.

Blackstone, William T. *Political Philosophy: an Introduction.* New York: Thomas Y. Crowell, 1973.

Bowen, Catherine D. *Miracle at Philadelphia: The Story of the Constitutional Convention, May to September 1787.* Boston: Atlantic Monthly Press, Little Brown, 1966.

——. *The Lion and the Throne: The Life and Times of Sir Edward Coke.* Boston: Atlantic Monthly Press, Little Brown, 1956.

Boyd, Julian P. *The Murder of George Wythe, Two Essays.* Williamsburg: Institute of Early American History and Culture, 1955.

Bridenbaugh, Carl. *Mitre and Sceptre: Transatlantic Faiths, Ideas, Personalities, and Politics, 1689–1775.* New York: Oxford University Press, 1962.

Brinton, Howard. *Friends for 300 Years: The history and beliefs of the Society of Friends since George Fox started the Quaker Movement.* New York: Harper & Brothers, 1952.

Brydon, George M. *Virginia's Mother Church,* vol. 1, 1607–1727, Virginia Historical Society, 1947; vol. 2, 1727–1814. Church Historical Society, 1952.

Catterall, Helen T., ed. *Judicial Cases concerning American Slavery and the Negro.* Vol. 1. Washington: The Carnegie Institution of Washington, 1926.

Clarkin, William. *Serene Patriot: A Life of George Wythe.* Albany: Alan Publications, 1970.

"Class Struggle and the American Revolution," *William and Mary Quarterly,* 3d ser., 13 (April, 1956.)

Cooley, Thomas M. "Copious Analysis of the Contents": *Commentaries on the Laws of England in Four Books* by Sir William Blackstone. 4th ed. Chicago: Callaghan, 1899.

Fleming, Thomas, ed. *Benjamin Franklin: A Biography in His Own Words.* New York: Newsweek, 1972.

Friends, London Yearly Meeting of the Religious Society. *Christian faith and practice in the experience of the Society of Friends.* London: Headley Brothers Ltd., 1960.

Gowans, Alan. *Images of American Living: Four Centuries of Architecture and Furniture as Cultural Expression.* Philadelphia: Lippincott, 1964.

Grigsby, Hugh Blair. *The History of the Virginia Federal Convention of 1788.* 2 vols. Richmond: Virginia Historical Society, 1890.

———. (Discourses) *The Life and Character of the Honorable Littleton Waller Tazewell,* 1860; *The Virginia Convention of 1776,* 1855.

Hemphill, W. Edwin. *Examinations of George Wythe Swinney for forgery and murder.* Williamsburg: Institute of Early American History and Culture, 1955.

———. "*George Wythe, America's First Law Professor and the Teacher of Jefferson, Marshall and Clay.*" Master's thesis, Emory University, 1933.

———. "George Wythe the Colonial Briton: A Biographical Study of the Pre-revolutionary Era in Virginia." Ph.D. dissertation, University of Virginia, 1937.

Herrink, L. S. *George Wythe* (The John P. Branch Historical Papers of Randolph-Macon College). Richmond: Richmond Press, 1912.

Hindle, Brooke. *The Pursuit of Science in Revolutionary America, 1735–1789.* Chapel Hill: The University of North Carolina, 1956.

Howison, Robert R. *A History of Virginia from its Discovery and Settlement by Europeans to the Present Time.* Richmond: Drinker and Morris. New York & London: Wiley and Putnam, 1848.

Irwin, Graham W., ed. *Harper Encyclopedia of the Modern World.* New York: Harper & Row, 1970.

Jefferson, Thomas. *Notes on the State of Virginia.* Chapel Hill: University of North Carolina Press, 1954. (See *Writings of T. Jefferson.* Ed. by A. A. Lipscomb, 20 vols. Washington, D. C., 1904–5).

———. *The Papers of.* 17 vols. Edited by Julian P. Boyd. Princeton: Princeton Press, 1950.

Kammen, Michael G. ed. "Virginia at the Close of the Seventeenth Century: An Appraisal of James Blair and John Locke." *Virginia Magazine of History and Biography* 74, 1966.

Ketcham, Ralph. *James Madison: A Biography.* New York: Macmillan, 1971.

Kimball, Fiske. *Domestic Architecture of the American Colonies and of the*

Early Republic. New York: Dover Publications, 1950.

Mays, David J. *Edmund Pendleton. A Biography,* 1721–1803. 2 vols. Cambridge: Harvard University Press, 1952.

Meade, Robert D. *Patrick Henry,* 2 vols. Philadelphia: Lippincott; vol. 1, 1957; vol. 2, 1969.

Meade, Bishop William. *Old Churches and Families of Virginia,* 2 vols. Philadelphia: Lippincott, 1857.

Miller, Helen H. *The Case for Liberty.* Chapel Hill: The University of North Carolina, 1965.

Munford, George Wythe. *The Two Parsons.* (excerpt) Richmond: J. D. K. Sleight, 1884.

Norton, John. *John Norton and Sons Papers.* Williamsburg: Colonial Williamsburg.

Pearson, Michael. *Those Dammed Rebels: The American Revolution As Seen Through British Eyes.* Toronto: Longmans, 1972.

Peterson, Merrill D. *Thomas Jefferson and the New Nation: A Biography.* New York: Oxford University Press, 1970.

Quarles, Benjamin. *The Negro in the American Revolution.* Chapel Hill: University of North Carolina Press, 1961.

Robert, Joseph C. *The Story of Tobacco in America.* Chapel Hill: University of North Carolina Press, 1949.

Rouse, Jr., Parke. *James Blair of Virginia.* Chapel Hill: University of North Carolina Press, 1971.

————. *Planters and Pioneers: Life in Colonial Virginia.* New York: Hastings House, 1968.

Russell, John H. *The Free Negro in Virginia, 1619–1865.* Baltimore: Johns Hopkins University Press, 1913.

Sanderson, John. *Biography of the Signers to the Declaration of Independence.* 9 vols. Philadelphia: Pomeroy, 1823–27.

Shewmake, Oscar L. *The Honorable George Wythe, Teacher and Lawyer, Jurist, Statesman.* (Address delivered in Williamsburg before the Wythe Law Club of the College of William and Mary, 1921.)

Smith, Page. *John Adams.* 2 vols. Garden City: Double Day, 1962.

Stanard, Mary Newton. *Colonial Virginia: Its People and Customs: Richmond, Its People And Its Story.* Philadelphia: Lippincott, 1923.

Starkey, Marion L. *The First Plantation: History of Hampton and Elizabeth City County, Virginia 1607–1887.* Hampton: Houston Printing and Publishing House, 1936.

Stoutamire, Albert. *Music of the Old South: Colony to Confederacy.* Cranbury: Fairleigh Dickinson University Press, 1972.

Todd, H. J., ed. *The Life and Designs of The Reverend Thomas Bray, D. D.* London, *1808*.

Tyler Papers, Archives, College of William and Mary.

Tyler, Lyon G., *Encyclopedia of Virginia Biography.* 5 vols. New York: Lewis, 1915.

———. *History of Hampton and Elizabeth City County.* 1922.

———. "The College of William and Mary: Its Work, Discipline, and History, from its Foundation to the Present Time." *Bulletin of the College of William and Mary* (May 1917).

Vaughan, Alden T., and Billias, George A. *Perspectives on Early American History: Essays in honor of Richard B. Morris.* New York: Harper & Row, 1973.

Whiffen, Marcus. *The Public Buildings of Williamsburg: Capital of Virginia.* Williamsburg: Colonial Williamsburg, 1958.

Wilbur, Earl M. *A History of Unitarianism in Transylvania, England and America.* Cambridge: Harvard, 1952.

Wilstach, Paul. *Tidewater Virginia.* New York: Tudor, 1945.

Wynne, F. H. "Dove Memorandum," 1856. BR Box 133, The Huntington Library.

Wythe, George. *Decisions of Cases in Virginia by the High Court of Chancery, with Remarks upon the Decrees by the Court of Appeals Reversing Some of Those Decisions.* Richmond, 1852.

INDEX